BUSES

YEARBOOK 2006

Edited by STEWART J. BROWN

Ian Allan
PUBLISHING

BUSES

YEARBOOK 2006

Contents

First published 2005

ISBN 0 7110 3054 5

© Ian Allan Publishing Ltd 2005

Published by Ian Allan Publishing

an imprint of Ian Allan Publishing Ltd, Hersham, Surrey KT12 4RG.
Printed in England by Ian Allan Printing Ltd, Hersham, Surrey KT12 4RG.

Code: 0508/E2

Front cover:
By the end of 2005 London's bus fleet was expected to be 100% low-floor. Among the earliest such double-deckers were Arriva's Alexander-bodied DAF DB250s. This 1999 10.2m-long example is seen at Brixton in 2003. *Gavin Booth*

Back cover (upper):
In recent years Scotland's bus fleets have undergone considerable change. The current generation of Stagecoach Bluebird buses includes TransBus Pointer Darts, as seen here in Inverness in 2004.

Back cover (lower):
During its short existence TransBus developed new designs to replace the existing Dennis range. A prototype Enviro200 midibus — with Alexander Dennis badge — is seen on trial with London United in February 2005. *Mark Lyons*

Title page:
Despite being part of TransBus, Plaxton continued to build bodies on rival manufacturers' chassis. Lothian Buses bought seven President-bodied Volvo B7TLs, of which this is one. *Plaxton*

Two Davids, Three Johns and Two Brians

Buses editor ALAN MILLAR relates the mixed fortunes of the businesses that came together briefly as TransBus International.

Some of the best stories about buses and bus manufacturers are about the people who took the decisions that determined the fates of their models. The story of the short reign of TransBus International, of its antecedents and hopefully long-lived successors is just such a tale. Hence its title.

It's a story of businesses that grew bigger in attempts to keep Britain among the dwindling number of nations with indigenous bus- and coach-manufacturing industries. A story that began with two Davids, more recently involved three Johns and is continuing with two Brians figuring alongside at least two other Davids (and doubtless several more Johns).

The two Davids were David Hargreaves and David Matthews, who successively expanded Hestair and Plaxton into bigger businesses intent on becoming world-class players.

When Hestair — the name is short for Heston Airport, which Hargreaves acquired in 1970 — bought Dennis Bros in 1972 the Guildford-based manufacturer was a shadow of its former self. Never much of a force in the postwar bus market, it had built its last Loline IIIs in 1967 and its last buses of any sort — dustcart-derived Pax Vs for Llandudno — a year later. You would have been excused for thinking then that it would never build another, yet by 1977 it had launched the Dominator double-decker and would follow it with a succession of cleverly conceived niche-market products. Market leader Leyland created many of the niches as it rationalised its range. Even so, when Hargreaves went on the record in a magazine article around then and said the ambition was for Hestair to

become the UK's biggest bus and truck builder this seemed more of a romantic dream than a realisable target.

It started off well by securing steady business from Leicester City Transport, whose General Manager — the legendary Geoffrey Hilditch — had bought the last Loline IIIs when he was in charge at Halifax. Another huge advance was to become the main supplier to South Yorkshire PTE, which almost alone wanted Rolls-Royce Eagle engines. And it grew big in the expanding market in Hong Kong. By being prepared to build bespoke buses Dennis gradually increased its market share. It even built a Dominator trolleybus for South Yorkshire in 1984.

The Hargreaves dream looked more like becoming reality in June 1983, when Hestair acquired Duple — by then very much the second force among British coach manufacturers. Once market leader, it had never fully recovered from its relocation to the old Burlingham plant in Blackpool, and the shortcomings of its products were being exposed by the veritable tide of imported coaches that reached our shores by the dawn of the 1980s. It had botched the launch of its new coach range — the oddly shaped Laser and hastily developed Caribbean — the previous autumn. But Hargreaves relished a basket-case and had proved with Dennis that such cases were by no means beyond salvation.

As Hestair Duple — Dennis by then was Hestair Dennis — it invested in a short-term revamp of the Laser and Caribbean and replaced them with new 300-series models in 1985. But there was little point in owning body- and chassis-manufacturing businesses unless you also intended to build

3

complete vehicles. Duple was already working on an integral Caribbean with Neoplan running units, but Hestair dropped that and instead produced the 425, a stunning-looking coach with Dennis running units.

These also were times of huge change for Dennis. Former Leyland man Steve Burton had joined as Production Director in 1982 and three years later took over Hargreaves's role as Managing Director. Under his guidance Dennis stepped away from building updated successors for other people's discontinued models and aimed to build larger volumes of standard products that nonetheless were highly innovative. First came the Javelin coach, in 1987, then the Dart midibus, two years later. As conceived, the Dart was available exclusively with a Duple body.

However, the Hargreaves years were ending. Hestair sold its vehicle-building businesses to a management buy-out in the name of Trinity Holdings at the beginning of 1989, and within months the new owners had taken their first tough decision. Duple — with no apparent prospect of recovery — would close, and Dennis would work instead with as many independent bodybuilders as possible. The one bit of Duple retained was Duple Metsec, the West Midlands-based manufacturer of body kits for export.

Left: The original Hestair concept was that the Dennis Dart would be a complete product with this style of body built by Duple, known as the Dartline. When Duple closed, Plaxton declined to buy the Dartline design, and it was sold instead to Carlyle — the former Midland Red central works — which built it in 1990/1 before going into liquidation. The Birmingham registration on this Rossendale example helps identify it as a Carlyle product. *Cromweld*

Below: A Berkhof-bodied Dennis Javelin of Banstead Coaches, the Surrey independent. Despite earlier fears for its future, Ministry of Defence orders have kept the Javelin in production. *Berkhof*

Above: Plaxton's move into the mainstream market depended partly on the success of the full-size Verde, which was launched in 1991. This is one of a small batch of Dennis Lances bought from stock by British Bus for its North Western fleet. Neither the Verde nor the Lance was particularly successful for its manufacturer. *Dennis*

Right: Typical of Northern Counties products when Henlys took over was the Palatine II double-decker. This is a Volvo Olympian for Bullock's of Cheadle, its livery clearly inspired by that of Travel West Midlands. *Northern Counties*

And this is where we catch up with the second David. For the Duple coach range was sold to David Matthews's Plaxton, a business he was intent on transforming into the big new force in the UK bus and coach market. Matthews had hit the ground running in 1987 when his Kirkby Central coach/truck/car-dealership business took over Plaxton and began stirring up a sleeping giant. Plaxton had prospered while Duple declined, but it was also suffering badly from foreign competition.

The new owner, a miner's son with a taste for saloon-car racing, intended to turn the tables on the importers by making Plaxton stronger at home and a big player in Europe. That meant building a full range of buses as well as coaches, it meant building better coaches, and it meant forging alliances with the big names in European chassis manufacturing. The company bought Carosserie Lorraine, a loss-making French coachbuilder, from Iveco (later using it to build a dozen Plaxton-badged versions of the Duple 425 for the UK) and also struck a deal with Mercedes-Benz to body O303 coaches, the intention being to build on both of these relationships.

Matthews pursued his bus ambitions by exploring the possibilities of buying Leyland Bus, Alexander, Northern Counties and the Metro-Cammell-Weymann Metrobus but ended up letting Plaxton develop its own single-deck citybuses. By the late-1980s the privatised operating industry was showing new interest in 11m-plus single-deckers, and Plaxton's priority was to develop its own, which appeared in 1991 as the Verde. Out of this — and first into production, at the start of the year — came the Pointer body, developed originally for the Dennis Dart by Reeve-Burgess, the company's small-bus/coach subsidiary. The new Premiere and Excalibur coaches followed that same autumn.

The pieces of the jigsaw were coming together, but (to mix metaphors) the wheels were also coming off the Matthews wagon. The economy was in recession, and orders were not coming fast enough to satisfy the City. Profitable Reeve-Burgess production was transferred to the main Scarborough plant to keep it going, and Carosserie Lorraine was closed in 1992. Matthews himself was squeezed out of the business at the end of 1991, and under new Chief Executive Robert Wood the parent company became Henlys, the name of its then car-dealership division.

The Matthews era wasn't quite over, as — perhaps embittered by the events of the previous year — he supported a hostile bid by Cowie (today's Arriva) to take over Henlys; should Cowie succeed, he would buy back Plaxton and merge it with at least one of the other surviving bus bodybuilders, to create a stronger business. In the event, Cowie's bid failed, Matthews remained in the wilderness and Robert Wood oversaw major expansion in 1995, when Henlys moved into North America in partnership with Volvo and at home bought Northern Counties from its management, at last providing Plaxton with double-deck-bodybuilding capacity.

That also was the year when two of the three Johns entered the picture. John Simpson was the charismatic Chairman of Mayflower, a Stock Market-listed automotive-engineering group that spotted an opportunity to expand into the bus market. John Fleming was one of his right-hand men. The opportunity they seized was to buy Alexander, then the world's largest volume builder of double-deck bodies for the UK and Far East markets. It was the latter market that particularly excited the two Johns.

Back in 1990 Alexander had been bought from its founding family by an outside team of manufacturing managers who broadened the product range and forged a good business relationship with Stagecoach, one of the emerging giants of the privatised bus industry. It helped that Alexander and Stagecoach both were based in Scotland and that Stagecoach's Brian Souter (yes, he is one of the two Brians who figure larger later in this story) is a patriot who, whenever it makes sense, tries to buy British — or, better still, Scottish.

At the time of the Mayflower takeover Alexander lacked any products in the fast-emerging new market for low-floor buses. By the end of 1996 it had unveiled, either in the metal or as drawings, the ALX200, ALX300, ALX400 and export ALX500 bodies to meet that requirement. Many of the home-market models would go to Stagecoach.

Just to remind ourselves, by 1998 Mayflower owned Alexander, with bodybuilding plants in Falkirk and Belfast. Henlys owned Plaxton, with bodybuilding plants in Scarborough, Wigan (ex-Northern Counties) and Anston, South Yorkshire; it also had the former Kirkby coach dealership at Anston. Both saw advantages of building complete vehicles, as Hestair/Trinity had done for six years in the 1980s, and both saw one obvious way of short-cutting the process: buying Dennis, which was building chassis in a modern plant at Guildford.

It made particular sense for Henlys, as Plaxton bodied the vast majority of the huge numbers of Dennis Darts being built. Such was the volume of Pointer-bodied Darts coming out of Scarborough that it was hard for other bodybuilders to compete on price or delivery, and the number of Pointers on other chassis — just Volvo's none-too-successful B6 and B6LE — was infinitesimal by comparison. Henlys tabled a friendly bid to buy Dennis and formalise what already was a close business relationship.

One potential complication was Henlys' relationship with Volvo. Besides being the 51% shareholder in the joint venture to buy Canadian manufacturers Prévost Car and NovaBUS, Volvo also had what it liked to describe as a 10% investment shareholding in Henlys. Most of Plaxton's coach output was on Volvo chassis. There was a suspicion in some quarters — mainly rival manufacturers — that Dennis would sooner or later be subsumed into a greater Volvo, but this still looked like a good deal for Plaxton and Dennis.

Mayflower now came in with a series of bids that ultimately scared off Henlys. It paid £275 million for Dennis — more than 10 times what it had cost to buy Alexander — and gained the means not only of building complete buses but also of offering chassis

Right: When Mayflower revamped the Alexander range the Mercedes Vario-based Sprint body gave way to the new ALX100, of which this Stagecoach Oxford vehicle — photographed in Chipping Norton — is an example.
Oxfordshire County Council

Left: Between its launch in late 1996 and the formation of TransBus four years later Alexander made considerable strides with the ALX200-bodied Dart SLF. First took several, including this one operating in Halifax.
Alexander

Right: A sizeable proportion of ALX400 bodies has been built on Volvo B7TL chassis, including this London Central example. *Volvo*

Above: The Dennis Dart SLF/Plaxton Pointer 2 combination was one of the British bus-manufacturing industry's biggest success stories of recent years — hence Plaxton owner Henlys' interest in merging with Dennis. This is one of many for FirstGroup, in the Provincial livery used before corporate 'Barbie' liveries took over. *Plaxton*

Below: Typical of the packaged products that TransBus was able to supply, a Plaxton President-bodied Dennis Trident in Brighton & Hove's Metro Line 5 livery. *TransBus*

and body together as complete, competitive packages. The ALX200-bodied Dart began to challenge the Dart/Pointer combination, which remained a strong force in the field; it also formed the basis of a bus that would take Mayflower into the North American bus market, in partnership with DaimlerChrysler's Thomas Built Buses division.

Henlys had good cause to be worried, and it made two strategic moves. One, in 1999, was to spend the money it would have spent on Dennis — and then some — in paying £415 million for Blue Bird, the USA's largest manufacturer of yellow schoolbuses and similar vehicles. The other was to develop alternative products to the Dart, which it had good cause to fear might no longer be quite so available from Mayflower. Both deals benefited from financial and physical input from Volvo.

Besides giving Henlys an even bigger presence in North America the Blue Bird deal provided Henlys with chassis-engineering skills. Henlys also tapped into available expertise in Hungary, where it set up a chassis-development operation using people who had learned their craft in the days when Ikarus was the undisputed bus giant of the Communist world.

Out of this came two products. One was Bus2000, a new low-floor body developed initially on the Volvo B6BLE chassis. The other was the LMB (Low Mass Bus), a chassis similar to a short Dennis Dart but built by Blue Bird. The first LMBs, with Pointer bodies, were built in a unit within the

Scarborough factory site. Both the LMB and the Bus2000-like Blue Bird ULF remain in production in the USA, the LMB looking uncannily like a Mini Pointer Dart.

These projects, especially the venture into chassis building, were fraught with risks for Henlys. They were bound to be expensive, they would stand or fall depending on how well the chassis compared against the proven Dart, and they depended on securing big volumes of sales. On the other hand, they also threatened to undermine the two Johns' project at Mayflower, where work had begun on a new range of complete buses. The two businesses were either destined or doomed to merge.

The deal put together from August 2000 was a joint venture that reflected the relative sizes of the two partners. TransBus International was owned 70% by Mayflower and 30% by Henlys but from the outset was seen as a Mayflower company in which another PLC just happened to have a minority shareholding. Despite the second word in its name, TransBus wasn't obviously international. Mayflower's joint venture to build what by then was the Thomas Dennis SLF200 in the USA was excluded, as were Henlys' ventures on that side of the Pond. TransBus continued to sell double-deckers in Hong Kong and expanded into the New York sightseeing-bus market, but outside Spain (where it enjoyed some small-scale gains) its ambitions in mainland Europe went largely unrealised.

From the beginning the outside view was that TransBus couldn't possibly sustain all of its inherited production capacity. When it first called in the bus and coach press to set out its plans at the beginning of 2001 few would have been surprised had the day's agenda included a briefing on why the Belfast and Wigan body plants would close. The greater surprise was that they wouldn't be closed.

The message then was also that TransBus would merely be the name of the holding company behind three established, well-respected brand names. Dennis, Plaxton and Alexander would live on, certainly for as long as the existing product ranges were produced. That message owed much to the

third John — John Smith, TransBus's first Chief Executive. He had been Dennis's Managing Director for lengthy spells beforehand and had seen how his company benefited while Leyland discarded its subsidiary brand names a quarter-century earlier. However, he retired in 2002, and it wasn't long before TransBus ousted the old brands on the grounds that none of the old names carried much recognition outside the UK.

Another TransBus message was that it still wanted to body other manufacturers' chassis. It had to say as much, for the Scarborough coach plant bodied relatively few chassis other than Volvos, and all three of the bus-body plants relied on Volvo (two of them also on smaller volumes of DAFs) for their survival. But it's no coincidence that Volvo, in particular, increased its co-operation with Wrightbus and East Lancs after TransBus came into being.

The first TransBus product to appear, in October 2001, was the Enviro300 single-decker. Truth be told, it was more like the first product of Mayflower's acquisition of Dennis. It grew out of a project (called SD99) to build a full-size, medium-weight counterpart of the ALX200-bodied Dart. The running units were beefed up equivalents of those in the Dart, while the main body structure — especially

Below: After a slow start Enviro300 sales began to pick up during 2004, new customers including Cardiff Bus, which already ran various lengths of Pointer Dart. *Mark Lyons*

Left: The first of 50 Enviro500 double-deckers for Las Vegas.
Alexander Dennis

the sides — was derived from the ALX300, which Alexander built on Volvo, MAN and DAF chassis. The one major Henlys contribution was that the front and rear ends were those developed for Bus2000.

The Enviro300 prototype appeared with Dennis badges, and early production models had Dennis branding on their steering-wheel centres, but from the outset this was promoted as a TransBus product.

When TransBus took its axe to production capacity in 2002 the victim was perhaps unexpected — not one of the apparently duplicated bus-body plants but the Plaxton site in Scarborough. The first announcement — which many believe was more of a negotiating ploy than a definite plan — was that the plant would close altogether. Coach production, if it was to survive, would go abroad, probably to Hungary, and production of the Pointer bus would move to Falkirk.

Within weeks a deal had been done to restructure working arrangements, and coach production remained on a scaled-down basis, with flexible labour agreements. That included a return to the traditional 'seaside' way of building coaches — shedding labour temporarily in the summer, when seasonal jobs are available in the leisure and catering industry. The man given the job of running

the new set-up was the other Brian — Brian Davidson, a young Scottish manager recruited initially at Alexander.

In little more than a dozen years the Scarborough plant was back where it had been when David Matthews first bought Plaxton — building coaches (mostly in the winter and spring) and focusing solely on meeting the needs of its market; it could no longer mask coach-manufacturing inefficiencies behind the efficiency of turning out hundreds of Pointer buses. The switch of Pointer production finally killed off the ALX200 in the UK, although it lives on in North America — now as an exclusively DaimlerChrysler product, with a Mercedes engine.

TransBus followed the Enviro300 with the tri-axle Enviro500 export double-decker — essentially a rationalised Trident/Alexander product designed as one vehicle — and in September 2003 unveiled prototypes of the Enviro200 midibus. This had an innovative rear exit, offside engine, full low-floor and Super Single rear wheels; there was even an Enviro200H diesel-electric hybrid, for which Go-Ahead signed a letter of intent to buy 12.

Briefing the press when the Enviro200 was unveiled, Mayflower's John Fleming was adamant that there were no plans to close any of the plants, even though the market was taking a sharp downturn following the end of London's buying

Above: A prototype Enviro200 — with Alexander Dennis badge — on trial with London United in February 2005. *Mark Lyons*

spree and the fruits of Volvo's co-operation with other bodybuilders were winning sales for rival manufacturers. Indeed, on the same day that Fleming was insisting on the 'no closures' line the press was taken around a Wigan plant so short of work that it was down to just one (albeit very efficient) production line. And we learned that Brian Souter's Stagecoach had brought forward a substantial order to throw TransBus a much-needed lifeline.

Two other factors were working against TransBus. One was that the reputation of Cummins, which supplied all the engines in TransBus chassis, wasn't all that it had been before, and this seemed to be especially the case when it came to after-sales support. The other was self-inflicted. In order to keep its many body plants as full as possible it was going out of its way to discourage customers from buying its chassis with other people's bodywork; following the collapse of Marshall Bus it cut off the supply of Dart chassis to successor company MCV. Other bodybuilders may not have been treated so harshly, but they didn't detect the co-operation they had enjoyed when Dennis was a free agent.

Not that any of this was unique to TransBus. Leyland had done much the same 20 years earlier as it struggled to maintain surplus production

capacity. Deals to buy, for example, ECW-bodied Olympians were far more tempting than those involving independent bodybuilders.

Fleming's 'no closures' claim seemed even less sustainable the morning after his briefing, when news broke in the Scottish press of a plan for a new plant in Falkirk. This new site would be big enough to absorb the work at every other one of the bus-body and chassis plants, but the official line remained as before: the superplant would replace only the existing Falkirk operations.

While all of this was going on Mayflower was quietly staving off a financial crisis induced in part by the colossal cost of servicing the loans to buy Dennis. Most of the property — not Falkirk, but including Guildford — was sold and leased back. Pension funds were diverted. And all the while the market was slowing down, for all the reasons already stated. By early 2004 a series of profits warnings was ringing alarm bells, and by the end of March the Good Ship Mayflower was heading rapidly for the rocks. John Fleming and John Simpson resigned just before the company was declared insolvent. TransBus was among the subsidiaries placed in administration — allowing it to continue trading pending a rapid sale.

The rumour-mill went into overdrive as the names of various potential buyers flew into and out of the frame. At one point it looked like Greencool, a Chinese company interested in exporting the know-how and technology, but in the end it was the two Brians who rode to the rescue and bought the business in its two obvious parts.

Within six weeks of the collapse Plaxton re-emerged as an independent company, with Brian Davidson as Chief Executive. He had left TransBus during one period of corporate disenchantment but had been persuaded to return to head up its after-sales business in the autumn of 2003. The new company — with the Scarborough plant, the Anston plant and dealership and the after-sales glass-replacement business — not only rejoiced in its old name but even revived a version of its pre-Matthews-era castle logo.

In fact the Plaxton name had never quite died. TransBus corporate policy had declared a *fatwa* on the P-word (along with the D-word and the A-word), but Scarborough seemed to get around that by having a copious supply of Plaxton-embossed rear-numberplate holders that continued to go on the backs of its coaches. It was little but important things like that which helped provide the new Plaxton with the sentimental support it needed from the coach-operating industry.

It took another week for the bus side to find its salvation. Journalistic licence says this is when Brian Souter rode to the rescue, but he wasn't alone. He was one important part of a consortium of Scotland's Great and Good. He and his sister, Ann Gloag, together owned 30% of the new company. David Murray, a leading businessman with a metals company that supplied Falkirk with raw materials, owned another 30%, and the Edinburgh-based Noble Grossart merchant bank held the other 40%. They, too, went for the old brand names and called their company Alexander Dennis.

The key managers brought in to run it were Bill Cameron and Jim Hastie, who had run Alexander in

Below: Artist's impression of an Enviro400 in Stagecoach livery.
Alexander Dennis

the earlier Mayflower years. Hastie quit when the TransBus deal was signed, arguing that the new business would be too big to survive. Few would dispute that he was right.

Alexander Dennis declined to buy the Belfast plant, which closed as orders were fulfilled. Contrary to expectations it took Wigan, which enjoyed a far better reputation for build quality and customer service than did Falkirk. As those final Stagecoach orders with TransBus were completed some ALX400s were assembled at Wigan, which until then had built only the former Plaxton President. However, a rapid business review confirmed what TransBus should have done all along. There wasn't enough work at home or abroad for all the plants, and especially those on expensive lease-back arrangements. Wigan would close early in 2005, once the last London orders for Presidents had been completed.

The early signs have been encouraging for both companies. Plaxton has revived the Mercedes-Benz Sprinter-based Pronto minibus that sputtered into life in the last days of TransBus. It has also been working on the core coach range and has adapted its Mercedes Vario-based Beaver midi to comply with the Disability Discrimination Act.

Alexander Dennis has at last begun to sell more respectable numbers of Enviro300s, is closer to putting the diesel version of the Enviro200 into production and has been working flat-out on a new Enviro400 double-decker. Tantalising drawings — and the real buses may well have appeared before you read this — suggest some adventurous styling to match the leadership that Wrightbus has set in this key market sector. And it has been working hard to sell the Enviro500 to new American customers, notably in Las Vegas.

But the challenges remain. For the competition isn't standing still. Besides the Volvo/Wrightbus combination, Scania has been moving fast in the double-deck market — with East Lancs, on its own and soon with Wrightbus — and all the while operators' confidence in what now is Alexander Dennis has been challenged by the events of 2004. Many worry that the company might not be around in its present form to support buses they hope to be running until 2020. For the sake of British manufacturing, we can only hope that the two Brians — and the many others at Alexander Dennis and Plaxton — convince them that the businesses once run by two Davids and later by three Johns will have a long and prosperous future.

Below: Plaxton remains in the bus market with the Beaver 2-bodied Mercedes-Benz Vario, of which Western Greyhound, in Cornwall, owned 36 by March 2005. *Plaxton*

Above: Plaxton's current range includes the Cheetah midicoach, based on the Mercedes-Benz Vario. *Plaxton*

Right: Artist's impression of the Plaxton Centro bus body, due to be launched in October 2005 on VDL SB120 and MAN 14.220 chassis. *Plaxton*

African AECs

For many years Britain's biggest bus makers were also major exporters. This was particularly true in the years following World War 2. STEWART J. BROWN illustrates AECs in South Africa.

Above: Johannesburg Municipal Transport was a major AEC customer and built up a fleet of over 100 Regent Vs with bodywork by Bus Bodies of Port Elizabeth. They entered service between 1957 and 1959. Note the battered front bumper in this 1976 view.

Right: Around the same time Johannesburg also had a small number of mid-engined Regals. The ornate gold fleet number would not have looked out of place on a British municipal bus. Note the unusual location for the route number, to allow space for twin destination blinds. The one blind in use shows the destination in English and Afrikaans.

Right: AEC supplied three-axle buses to South African operators in the 1970s. This is a front-engined Kudu, with a set-back axle to provide space for an entrance in the front overhang. It was in the municipally-owned Alberton fleet. Buses in South Africa had to display a notice indicating when they were full. The notice is displayed on this Kudu but seems to be a little inaccurate. The body was to the standard Bus Bodies design of the time.

Left: The Ranger, like the Kudu, was front-engined, but with a conventionally-located front axle, as seen on this Brakpan Municipality bus leaving the town's railway station.

Below: SMT — Springs Municipal Transport — was another AEC operator in the Greater Johannesburg area, with a fleet which included Kudus. AEC did considerably better than arch-rival Leyland in this region. The kudu is a breed of South African antelope.

Left: Ultimately, of course, Leyland took control of AEC, and this led to a period of so-called badge engineering. This 'Leyland' is in fact an AEC Kudu, operated by a Pretoria-based independent.

Right: East London Municipal Transport standardised on AECs in the 1950s but would later switch its allegiance to Mercedes-Benz. Its first postwar buses were Regals, and in a country where buses often had short lives by European standards some of the earliest Regals operated for almost 30 years.

Left: The front-engined Regals at East London were followed by batches of mid-engined Regal IVs, and these too were long-lived. One heads up the main street of East London in 1975, heading for the English-sounding suburb of Cambridge West.

Right: The purchase of RTLs in large numbers by Cape Tramways of Cape Town overshadowed the fact that a small number of London Transport RTs joined the East London fleet. These were rebuilt with front entrances but retained their rear staircases. Latterly they were devoted to school services.

Left: Front-engined buses were favoured throughout Africa because in most places much of their mileage was on dirt roads. A Kudu of the Ciskei Transport Corporation kicks up dust as it heads towards East London. To make its fleet appear bigger than it was CTC missed out alternate numbers.

Right: The ultimate indignity to AEC enthusiasts? This Alberton Kudu with Bus Bodies body has the AEC grille which was supplied with the chassis but instead of the famous 'blue triangle' badge at the top has Leyland lettering spread artistically — if not in a corporately approved style — across the grille.

No More Fares Please?

As the last Routemasters mark the end of crew operation on regular bus services in Britain, DAVID THROWER looks back at the colourful history of the conductor, for so long an integral part of public transport.

All photographs from the Museum of Transport Collection, Manchester, except where credited otherwise

For the enthusiast, the past couple of years have been dominated by the final decline of the Routemaster. But their demise marks another major change, of much wider importance to the general public — the end, to all intents and purposes, of the conductor.

In truth, much of Britain has now been without conductor-operated bus services for three decades, whilst rural bus services were moving towards one-man operation half a century ago. But the era of the conductor has nevertheless finally spanned a century-and-three-quarters, and for most of the past century has included conductresses.

Early days

The need for conductors arose with the coming of the pioneering horse-bus services during the late 1820s and 1830s. The novelty of these services, compared with long-distance stage-coaches and the local urban hackney coaches (or 'short stages'), which were for the well-off and only carried six passengers inside and a few more on top, was that they were larger and more comfortable than their predecessors, carrying 12 inside and three on top, and also picked up passengers at intermediate stops.

Changes in taxation in 1842, taxing vehicles rather than numbers of passengers carried, encouraged operators to enlarge omnibuses further, with operators fitting longitudinal 'knifeboard' seating along the roof and increasing payloads to about 22 passengers. All these larger vehicles required a second man, or sometimes only a boy, to travel, to supervise loading, and take the money. Thus the conductor — and the bus crew — was born.

By the early 1850s there were over 800 conductor-operated omnibuses working in London, and substantial fleets were working in other major cities. The low fares — the typical fare in London from Paddington to the City had progressively been cut from 1s 6d (7.5p) in short-stage days to only 3d (just over 1p) — brought transport within reach of the great majority, hence 'omnibus'. Consequent rapid growth in demand now meant that thousands of men were needed to work as conductors.

The first real attempt at regulating conductors, or 'directors', as they were sometimes also known, was an Act of Parliament passed in August 1838. Conductors (and drivers) working within 10 miles of London's General Post Office had to wear a metal badge bearing a number, so that any angry passengers could quote it when lodging complaints. By 1899 the number of licensed conductors in inner London alone had grown to nearly 9,000.

The early conductors were rough-and-ready characters, quick of wit and tongue. The satirical magazine *Punch* certainly railed against them during late 1849, complaining about the altercations over fares and demanding that fixed rates be published, rather than fares often being left to each passenger to acrimoniously negotiate with conductors, or 'cads', as they were termed. Punch wryly commented that it was ironic that conductors did not know how to conduct themselves.

Incidentally, the term 'conductor' seems to have originated from the concept that these men were conducting their employers' business. Their pay unfortunately included the calculation that conductors would probably make an extra five or six shillings a day on the side, over and above their wages. If they made less, they (or their families) went hungry. If they made too much more, they were sacked.

Above: A tram crew in Edwardian times — both male, of course. Their appearance changed little over half a century.

The motor-bus era, effectively commencing *c*1905, brought its own problems. The early designs had solid tyres, giving a hard ride over cobbles, and of course were open-top, with open staircases, giving virtually no protection to the hapless conductor in rain, wind and wintry weather. The electric trams, which had been so successfully introduced in such large numbers from the mid-1890s, also still had open tops until the early years of the 20th century, when operators started to experiment with covered tops. The difficulties of collecting fares upstairs on an open-topper in gas-lit streets and biting cold can only be imagined.

By the late 1930s most open-top buses and trams had been either enclosed or withdrawn and scrapped, but the privations of conductors being exposed to the weather were to end only with the withdrawal of the very last open-staircase buses in the late 1940s. Even then, the provision of saloon heaters was far from universal until as late as the 1960s, and many conductors on open-platform buses could only stamp their feet during winter weather. For a century, greatcoats, scarves and gloves (usually with the fingers cut off) remained essential for conducting in winter, and standing (or, worse still, sitting) in the lower saloon, to shelter from the cold, was usually strictly forbidden.

In country areas in winter, conductors might also have to help dig their buses out of the snow. But pride in the job, in an era when travellers had little alternative transport (other than the railways and the pedal-cycle), always shone through.

Fare collection

Initially, fare-collecting by conductors involved no more than an outstretched hand. But petty fraud was so rampant during Victorian times, and concern at lost takings so great, that a proper fare-collecting system had to be devised.

An ingenious early system was Kaye's Patent Fare Collector, introduced during the 1870s, whereby money was posted by the passenger through a top slot into a transparent hand-held box. If the fare was agreed as being correct, the conductor then depressed a plunger on the box, and the coins dropped through into a locked compartment. Interestingly, this concept was to reappear in the 1960s with the 'Johnson Box' on one-man buses.

With the Kaye system, conductors were also given a change float, but this was kept separate, and they were not allowed to handle the final fare. There was also an oil-lamp for conductors to use at night, and carrying a nearly full Kaye machine plus lamp on a moving bus or tram, without either dropping the machine or burning oneself or the passenger, must have been tricky.

By far the most popular conductors' ticket-issue device, widely introduced during the late 19th century, was to be the Bell Punch system, with racks of pre-printed card tickets, serially numbered, and with the machine's distinctive 'ting' as each ticket was cancelled during issue. In Liverpool the early punch system incorporated a counter, creating a simple cash-register. Belfast Corporation used a similar system. Another very early ticket-canceller was the Barker, a squat and heavy circular machine, and Williamson's also made machines very similar to those of Bell Punch.

On a large provincial-city operation, between 100 and 150 million tickets might be issued each year, every one having to be accounted for manually. The Bell Punch concept would ultimately last some 80 years, from the horse bus and horse tram to the 1950s, although in some fleets, such as Southern Vectis, it had given way by the 1930s to new technology (in that particular instance, to the 'Automaticket' system). London finally gave up the Bell Punch only in 1957.

By the Edwardian era conductors could be found working in their tens of thousands, on horse buses,

Above: Two youthful conductors carrying Williamson ticket machines are seen in 1913 alongside a pair of Oldham Corporation Tilling-Stevens double-deckers.

Left: Bus-conducting was thirsty work, and many a bus was delayed as the crew snatched a quick cup of tea between trips. These three gentlemen were tram pointsmen rather than conductors, but the picture catches the spirit of the times, as they have a drink in a bus converted to serve as a mess room.

London, 'If conductors run short of tickets during a journey, they must report the matter to the first Official (it was always a capital 'O') whom they see, borrow a supply from another conductor, and obtain a further supply from the Depot as soon as possible. They must subsequently report the matter on an Irregularity or Occurrence Report.'

Needless to say, there were plenty of other rules. Conductors couldn't smoke, least of all within the saloon. And so having a drag at the terminus, either standing around the front of the bus or in those cheap but cheerful cafés so beloved of bus and tram crews, became part of everyday bus life. Alcoholic drinking on duty had been outlawed, of course, but many busmen occasionally took a chance and quietly downed the odd pint when the opportunity arose, even if it risked serious trouble.

As well as the usual strictures about behaving 'in a civil and orderly manner', conductors were not allowed to speak to the driver when the vehicle was in motion 'unless necessary to do so in order to

the first motor buses, horse, steam and electric trams and even battery buses and the first trolleybuses, Bell Punch and cashbag strapped around them, ticket rack in hand and loose change jingling, with their immortal cries of "Any more fares?", "Move on down the bus", "Room for one inside" and "Hold very tight please!". With heavy passenger demand and full loads, short riders and universal cash fares, they often worked very hard, and from early 1914, in London at least, there were additional 'boy conductors' to help to reduce boarding accidents on busy routes.

The use of the ticket equipment spawned its own lengthy stream of rules and edicts. For example, in give direction as to the stopping of the vehicle'. There were also numerous other rules that the passengers were meant to (but all too often did not) observe, and the hapless conductor had to enforce these too, somehow ensuring that his precious cargo did not spit, smoke downstairs, harass one another, board moving vehicles or hurl objects from the windows.

Conductors didn't just have to collect fares and supervise the passengers. On remote routes, to save the cost of an inspector, roadside time-clocks were used, with conductors having to alight and punch a special card to record running times. In fact, the conductor was often technically in charge of the bus, even to the point where he or she was held responsible if a driver accidentally went off the normal line of route, or simply ran very early.

was once an essential (if minority) source of bus revenue and only really died out with the advent of one-man operation in the late 1960s.

Equipment

The equipment issued to conductors throughout Britain altered little during the latter part of the 19th century and the first half of the 20th. For example, from the 1920s to the 1950s the usual issue for London conductors and conductresses would include a leather moneybag, a mousetrap ticket rack, a Bell Punch machine and canceller mounted on a polished-metal backing-plate with harness, a locker key, a winding-handle (for tram destinations), a waybill clipboard and (for trams, at least) a whistle. Many operators also included this for bus conductors, for reversing at termini where there was no turning circle.

Left: The conductor was responsible for safety on the platform, ensuring that passengers got on and off without injury — which could be difficult when people tried to board a moving bus. This Central SMT Leyland Titan in Glasgow appears to be stationary. Once the passengers were on board the conductor would give two rings on the bell, signalling to the driver that it was safe to go.
Stewart J. Brown collection

Below: An Aberdeen Corporation conductor climbs back onto his AEC Regent III after stamping his time card at the clock by the bus stop near the outer terminus of the service to Northfield. *Stewart J. Brown*

Trolleybus conductors also had to leap off at junctions and run ahead to haul on a metal knob attached to trolleybus poles, to pull down the 'frog' on the wiring, where a vehicle had to diverge from the main line of route. Where de-wirings occurred, there was also the ritual of removing a 15ft bamboo pole from beneath the trolleybus and reuniting the trolleybus's boom with the overhead system. Tram conductors, of course, also had to do this at termini, where trams reversed, or occasionally if they de-wired.

With motor buses, conductors would even take charge of topping up radiators when leaving the garage, if only to help their mates. And country (and even some city) bus conductors had to take responsibility for parcels. The carriage of parcels

Whistles were also used on the upper decks of tramcars as a signal to start. Conductors on buses, trolleybuses and trams in the North of England were, incidentally, widely known as 'guards', this term lasting until bus deregulation, and the end of conducting, in the 1980s.

As for cash-bags, those in the know would always plump for a worn one rather than a new one, as the leather strap would be more supple and easier on the shoulder. And pre-decimal (pre-February 1971)

coinage was large and heavy. With large numbers of short-distance riders, bags could weigh the proverbial ton, and new conductors soon learned to dispense change as rapidly as they could spare it, building up banknotes and keeping their cash-bags as empty as they could. This also greatly speeded up paying-in at the end of each shift. Conductors always tried as far as possible to cash up during their last trip, occasionally forgoing the final few passengers' fares.

Left: A conductress with a Setright ticket machine stands alongside her driver beside an Alexander Leyland Titan, probably in the 1930s. *Stewart J. Brown collection*

Below: Three staff of the North Western Road Car Co pose beside a 1923 Brush-bodied Daimler Y-type. The conductor is wearing an ordinary cap rather than a standard-issue uniform item, as worn by his colleagues.

Each ticket machine usually had its numbered box. The Bell Punch ticket machine came in a leather-reinforced box about the size of a large shoebox, later varieties of machine often requiring rather larger cases, or, in the case of the Setright, a black or silver tin. These were also used to hold spare ticket rolls, spare waybills, farebooks, supplies of emergency tickets and 'budgie' (budget) keys for destination boxes, as well as paper bags to bag up money.

Conductors also had to record their ticket-stock numbers, or take down their machine's numbers, not just at the terminus but also at boundary-points between different operators on jointly worked services. And, of course, the cash had to match the ticket-machine readings or printed-ticket stocks, as any shortages ('shorts') would be deducted from their pay. In companies such as North Western, even in the 1950s, three incidences of shorts meant a dismissal. The legality of deducting shorts was questioned at times by the unions, as this practice penalised conductors for making honest mistakes and even for accepting counterfeit coins.

Uniform issue would include summer jackets and winter greatcoats, caps (sometimes with a white top), cap badge, PSV badge and staff pass (when these were issued), together with rule book. The conductor's symbol of office was the PSV-licence badge. From January 1935 the familiar circular green-bordered badges were introduced, displacing the oval enamel badges that had been issued since Victorian times. Conductors were required to wear badges until the Government finally abolished them in July 1980, although many of the by-then-dwindling numbers of conductors continued to display them, as part of their pride in the job.

Wartime working

Of all the periods in the history of bus conducting, none could match the intensity and drama of wartime. In fact there was eventually to develop a strong link between the armed services and bus crews, with many conductors and drivers enlisting during the two World Wars. Conversely, in the years after each war many new conductors and drivers joined the buses from the armed forces, having become well-used to being part of a disciplined uniformed workforce.

Wartime also brought about other rapid changes. The very first conductresses appeared in London during World War 1, in November 1915 on Thomas Tilling's route 37 through Richmond, Putney and Clapham, and by 1916 General was also actively advertising for conductresses, but they had to be at least 5ft tall and aged between 21 and 35 (although the notion of being refused employment because you were 36 years old, particularly during a time of national crisis, seems truly incomprehensible today).

By the end of 1916 General employed over 1,700 conductresses, mainly former domestic servants. Uniforms included felt hats and serge skirts and

Left: Probably set up as a wartime morale-booster, this picture shows two Manchester tram conductresses — or guards, as they were also known — in their Edwardian-style uniforms complete with smart new leather cash bags and Bell Punch ticket machines.

and public-transport staff found themselves on the front line. Conductors and drivers were constantly exposed to risk of death or injury during air raids, frequently shepherding their passengers to safety and then taking shelter themselves. Despite the risk of high-explosive and incendiary bombs and flying shrapnel, bus, tram and trolleybus crews often carried on working regardless, abandoning their vehicles only if bombing became intense.

World War 2 brought back conductresses. On London Transport, which recruited 11,250 clippies, they were given uniforms in grey worsted material with blue piping, marking them out from the men's navy-blue serge. Women also preferred trousers to skirts, for greater warmth in winter. Later all crews wore navy blue, bus conductresses having blue piping and tram conductresses red. Across the country thousands of women joined the buses; in some fleets, such as Southern National and Western National, the number of conductresses reached 90% of the total conducting staff.

Throughout the war conductors and drivers maintained a routine stoicism, trying to collect fares in the blackout, struggling to and from work through rubble-strewn streets and having to put up with missing or boarded-up windows in winter.

jackets for winter, with straw hats and 'dust-coats' for summer. Women working on the motor buses — and on the electric tramcars — worked 10-hour shifts, six days per week. The term 'clippie' also seems to date from this time. But conducting was still regarded as a man's job, and the last woman conductor in London lost her job in November 1919.

During World War 1 civilian air-raid casualties from Zeppelin attacks were modest, but World War 2 was to see widespread civilian carnage,

Far left: A newly trained conductress practises with her ticket machine, probably in the 1940s.

Left: A conductress with a rack of tickets, posing for a World War 2 publicity photograph.

Above: Conductors and conductresses were also responsible for the safety of passengers boarding and alighting from open-platform buses — and when the bus was full to prevent any more passengers boarding.

Above right: Ready for the road — four conductresses emerge from the training school to fill posts left vacant by men who had gone to fight in World War 2.

At the end of both World Wars, unbelievably, many conductresses were once again dismissed, simply because they were women and to provide jobs for returning ex-servicemen. Between May 1945 and December 1946 numbers in London fell from 10,000 to 4,000, despite their (but not their union's) resistance. They were soon back — staff shortages saw to that — as London Transport rescinded the planned replacement of women by men in February 1947. From the late 1940s conductresses became the norm all over Britain, though they were to be denied the opportunity of re-training as drivers, with their higher rates of pay, until the 1970s.

Later ticketing systems

By the 1950s a whole range of ticketing systems was in use. For example, across Middle England during the 1960s Colchester, Grimsby-Cleethorpes and Lowestoft used TIMs; Barton, Coventry, Eastern Counties, East Midland, Lincolnshire Road Car, Mansfield, Midland General, South Notts, Trent

and United Counties used Setrights, and Ipswich, Leicester, Lincoln, Northampton and Nottingham used Ultimates. Eastern National used a mixture of Setright and Almex, and West Bridgford used Ultimates and Almex. A few operators, such as Great Yarmouth, used three different systems, in this instance Setrights, TIMs and Ultimates.

Fare scales also became very complicated by this time, and the concept of crude leaps in fares (as practised today) would have been regarded as

Below: The conductor of a Liverpool Corporation Daimler has a quick smoke and a chat with his driver at Pier Head in 1963. The conductor has an Ultimate ticket machine. *Harry Hay*

Above: **By 1969 — the date of this photograph — little had changed in four decades. A conductor demonstrates a TIM machine. Note the leather-reinforced cuffs on his jacket.** *Oldham Evening Chronicle*

Right: **If an Alexander's conductor lost his Setright or TIM ticket machine — or 'register', as it was described in this notice — in 1947 it would cost him £15, deducted from his wages at the rate of 10s (50p) a week.**

completely unacceptable. There were early-morning and workmen's fares, through tickets for onward travel, cheap off-peak tickets, return tickets, tickets for children, tickets for blind people, minimum fares for express and limited-stop services, restrictions at peak times, tickets for dogs … the conductor had somehow to try to remember all these permutations, whilst avoiding undercharging (for which he or she could be booked, if caught by a revenue inspector) and possible disputes with passengers.

Big steps forward during the 1950s were the switch from Bell Punch/ Williamsons, Willebrews and 'insert' Setrights to Gibsons, Setright Speed and other self-totalling systems, dispensing at last with the cumbersome mousetrap ticket racks and blocks of card tickets, though some operators, such as Central SMT and North Western Road Car, carried on with the slower insert Setrights and Willebrews until the late 1950s and sometimes even

beyond. In the late 1960s Passenger Transport Executives, such as SELNEC and its successor, Greater Manchester, tried to sweep away their motley inheritance of ticketing systems, in this particular instance standardising on the Almex.

In fact, outside London the era of conductors using modern machines such as Almexes was short, mainly due to operators' dispensing with crew operation altogether but partly also due to the impending arrival of the electronic age. A further revolution occurred with London's dwindling numbers of conductors during the 1980s, when PETMs (portable electronic ticket machines) were introduced to replace the by-now-obsolete but much-loved Gibsons. It is remarkable to think of London moving from Bell Punch via Gibsons to mini-computers within the space of three decades.

Improving conditions

It is difficult to be precise about how much conductors earned during the 20th century, because rates of pay varied considerably across the country. Usually London led the way, and the 1930s also seemed generally to mark the high-point in the conductor's status. But even in London there was a strike in 1937, busmen being represented by the Transport & General Workers' Union, the Communist Party and the London Busmen's Rank-and-File Movement.

W. ALEXANDER & SONS, LIMITED

NOTICE regarding

DEDUCTIONS

from WAGES

IN COMPLIANCE WITH THE PROVISIONS OF THE TRUCK ACTS, WE HEREBY GIVE NOTICE THAT THE TERMS OF THE CONTRACT OF EMPLOYMENT BETWEEN US AND OUR DRIVERS AND CONDUCTORS, OR OTHER EMPLOYEES WHILE ACTING AS DRIVERS OR CONDUCTORS, INCLUDE AN AGREEMENT BY SUCH EMPLOYEES THAT THE FOLLOWING DEDUCTIONS SHALL BE MADE FROM WAGES :—

I. DRIVERS :

(1) Lost Radiator Cap	... ...	8/-
(2) Lost Petrol Cap	... ...	4/4
(3) Lost Oil Cap	... ...	2/8
(4) Broken window of door of driver's cab or wind-screen, if due to negligence		
	Driver's Cab	19/8
	Windscreen	23/6
(5) Premium for Life Insurance Scheme, where the employee has agreed to enter Scheme.		
(6) Contributions to hospitals or Infirmaries or other charitable objects to which the employee has agreed to contribute.		

II. CONDUCTORS :

(1) Any deficiency between the face value of tickets and cash supplied and the face value of tickets and cash accounted for.		
(2) In the case of used Return tickets collected by the conductor and thereafter lost or not accounted for, there shall be deducted from the conductor's wages one half of the face value of such tickets.		
(3) Premiums for Life Insurance Scheme	{ as detailed above under	
(4) Contributions to Hospitals, etc.	{ Drivers (5) and (6).	
(5) Lost Setright Register	... ...	£15*
(6) Lost T.I.M. Register	... ...	£15*

Right: Not all conducting duties were onerous. The conductress on this Alexander Northern Leyland Royal Tiger is applying destination bills — 'Aberdeen via Forfar' and 'Limited Stop' — to the windscreen. When the coach loads in Glasgow and she has checked the passengers' tickets, she will have little more work to do.
Stewart J. Brown

Below right: By the 1970s bus crews no longer wore caps; a few years earlier some operators would have reprimanded them for such behaviour. The conductor looks less than convinced that the potion produced by the Teamatic machine is indeed tea.

By 1951, for a 44-hour week covering six days, a London conductor in the Central Area would earn £6 6s (£6.30) during his or her first six months' service, rising to £6 9s (£6.45) for the next six months, then finally to £6 12s (£6.60) thereafter. By 1965 a conductor earned £17 12s 11d (£17.65) for an average week, excluding voluntary overtime. Provincial rates lagged a little behind London. By 1970 rates including overtime had reached £25 — higher than those for shop assistants but still far from generous.

There were also higher rates for working at certain times, for example on Sundays, Good Friday and Bank Holidays, when time-and-a-half rates applied, with a tempting offer of double time on Christmas Day. A conductor could also work overtime, if it was available, for which (in London, at least) anything over the standard 7hr 20min day was paid at time and a half. Such extras gradually spread across the UK through union bargaining. Amalgamations, such as into Passenger Transport Executives, usually boosted the poorer rates, through levelling-up.

Special rates also applied to early starts and late finishes. And 'early' and 'late' really did mean just that! A conductor in London in the 1950s would be paid an extra 2s (10p) for a duty that started before 4am, an extra 1s 6d (7½p) before 4.30am, an extra 1s (5p) for before 5am, and a bare 6d (2½p) extra if it was pre-6am. For a late finish (after 1am) it was an extra 2s (10p), and for a very late finish (after 2am) an extra 1s (5p). The rates sound mean and barely worth the bother by today's standards, but these were very good arrangements in comparison with those of small private provincial operators, where trade unions (if present at all) had much less bargaining power.

Another interesting aspect was that, for many years, equality of the sexes did not apply. For example, in the early 1950s in London new conductors received only 13s 4d (67p) per day during training or route-learning, and conductresses received 10% less than that, in other words just 12s (60p) per day. It was part of a culture of inequality that was to end only slowly, during the later 1950s and 1960s, culminating in the Equal Opportunities and Equal Pay Acts of 1974/5. Bus staff actually led the way in the area of equal pay. After all,

conductresses did their jobs just as well as the men, it was demonstrably exactly the same job, and trade-union membership gave them industrial muscle.

In fact, during the 1950s and 1960s women made up a large proportion of the conducting workforce. In Glasgow, for example, by 1961 there were 202 conductresses on the trams, compared with 175 conductors, and 181 conductresses on the trolleybuses, compared with 121 conductors. On the motor buses it was just about level pegging, with 1,032 women and 1,063 men. Interestingly, Glasgow's training school put through 743 conductresses that year, compared with 1,610 men, suggesting that the men tended to move on rapidly (or get sacked), whereas the women stuck the job for rather longer. But a few years later, by 1966, men were in the majority in Glasgow by a factor of three to two, women perhaps by then preferring employment in expanding retailing and light industry, which fitted in better with family life.

The 1960s also brought about the modernisation of the conductors' uniforms. Gone for ever were the 1930s-style greatcoats and heavy jackets, white-topped caps for men and caps or berets for women, and much else. In their place came smart short jackets and sometimes trendy pillbox hats. The mid-1960s London styles in particular were quite natty and looked almost as much a part of fashion as the mini skirt and Twiggy.

In retrospect, one of the more remarkable aspects was that many conductors put in such long years. In the late 1950s one West Ham trolleybus conductor, Henry Cruse, was still at work at the age of 77, having conducted for more than 40 years. A Dalston conductor went on record as having worked an incredible 53 years, starting with the earliest motor buses in 1911 and ending his career on Routemasters in the late 1960s.

Economies

The bus conductor and driver have always made up a significant percentage of the cost of running a bus, and ending the use of conductors was brought about by the need for economy. In fact, the move to one-man operation started back in the 1920s, and perhaps even earlier. Cardiff had one-man buses on quiet routes as early as 1923, as had many other operators.

Left: Drivers of one-man buses typically earned an extra 15% for the additional work involved. This is a Bolton Corporation Leopard in the mid-1960s, with a rather bemused-looking driver collecting a fare. *Stewart J. Brown collection*

Above right: The atmosphere of the crew canteen is captured in this 1960s view, in which you can almost hear the arguments — over shifts, overtime, the new depot inspector or last night's TV. A conductor keeps his hands warm on an enamel tea can.

By the 1960s the whole concept of having a conductor was under scrutiny. One 1969 study of 29 municipal operators concluded that a 14% saving could be made by switching to one-man operation, which at that time accounted for typically 20% of the route-network total.

The need for much more widespread economies was driven by a huge fall in patronage. In 1950 about 1,650 million local journeys were made by bus, trolleybus or tram, almost all of these services being crew-operated. By the end of the century that figure would fall to just over 400 million, and the economics of the remaining bus operations had altered out of all recognition.

Eliminating conductors meant paying part of the savings to drivers. In London in the late 1960s one-man drivers earned 15% more than their crew-operation counterparts, though this was a bare 5% on standee Red Arrow-type buses, on which passengers were supposed to put coins in a slot and pass through a turnstile.

Most operators outside London eliminated conductors and conductresses during the 1970s. For example, Lincoln City Transport's last went in 1978, and Lincolnshire Road Car's in 1982. The end of conductor operation was often marked in the local press. Occasionally, just a handful of the more elderly staff would work on for a few more months on modern buses, such as Leyland Nationals, until they retired. Many conductors re-trained as drivers, but some were too old or just didn't fancy one-man operation, seeing it as doing two jobs for one pay packet. Sometimes office jobs were found for those who couldn't re-train. But many simply retired early or left to seek other work.

Comedy turns

There has always been a strong link between bus conducting and comedy. It reached its high-point (or, arguably, low-point) with the television series *On the Buses*, courtesy of sitcom writers Wolfe and Chesney, and starring driver Stan Butler

(Reg Varney) and conductor Jack Harper (Bob Grant), together with the notorious "I 'ate you, Butler!" Inspector 'Blakey' Blake (Stephen Lewis). Both Grant and Lewis contributed scripts to the series, set at the fictitious Luxton & District Bus Company.

In fact, vulgar and corny as it was, *On the Buses*, filmed at Eastern National's Wood Green garage, was an extraordinary commercial success, perhaps the last fling of the 1950s British comedy genre, although it came rather late — like the buses it portrayed. It resulted in a creditable 74 TV episodes, lasting until 1975, plus three full-length cinema films, *On the Buses* (1971), *Mutiny on the Buses* (1972) and *Holiday on the Buses* (1973). And the films were very popular, the 1971 production being the top British box-office hit for that year, even outpacing James Bond. It wasn't to everyone's taste, but it was the British bus conductor's highest profile ever and now seems set to immortalise the job for all time.

Apparently, the BBC had disdainfully turned down the embryonic TV series. The equally lordly London Transport had also refused to co-operate, fearing that its corporate image would be debased. LT's letter of refusal was ceremonially framed and hung on the wall in London Weekend Television's production office!

These celluloid comedies doubtless stretched credibility, but they captured that essential feature of bus-conducting, that of having a good time and larking about just as much as one could get away with, passing the day with a rapid-fire wit and endless banter whilst avoiding the eagle eye of authority. It was a sort of morality play in reverse, where the bus crews misbehaved and got away with it, perhaps creating an unintended historical echo of the 'cads' of early Victorian days.

Comedians Eric Sykes and Hattie Jacques also depicted bus work in their 1973 TV series. Another comedian on the buses was Spike Milligan, appearing working as a conductor but dressed as Richard III. (In another sketch Milligan sits in a Chinese restaurant and says "I'll have a number 19", whereupon an RT on route 19 comes clean through the restaurant wall!)

In truth, the antics of *On the Buses* were all too often acted out in real life. Buses leaving their conductors behind, buses going round roundabouts three times to throw off the one behind, romances on the buses, all were true.

And there were endless bizarre incidents, mostly due to the vagaries of the Great British Public. One conductor in the Thames Valley had a passenger board the bus with half-a-dozen swans. Then there was the conductor who, travelling in thick fog near Chatham, suddenly found himself surrounded by cows, his driver having gone right off the road and into a farmyard, demolishing a cowshed. Another conductor, working an open-top bus on route 8 across Central London in the late 1920s, was collecting fares at the front of the upper deck when up the stairs came two men leading a donkey. Unsurprisingly, there was no removing it, and the bus went through Oxford Street and all the way to Willesden with the donkey noisily hanging its braying head over the side of the bus.

Some conductors were made of tougher stuff. The immortal Glaswegian conductress's line, "C'mon an' gerroff!" comes to mind. And you had to be pretty tough, on a late-night bus in Glasgow, Newcastle or any large city that functioned on alcohol after 8pm on a Friday or Saturday night. Official advice was to use the ticket machine as a weapon if all other reasoning failed, and, whatever you did, not to get off the bus. But the best strategy was always to adopt a cheery outlook and avoid getting into disputes.

Last stand

In 1980, when conductors had all but disappeared from most of the rest of Britain, London Transport still employed more than 7,000. But the Routemaster run-down in London in the mid-1980s saw the end of conductors in outer London and on many of the less-lucrative inner-London routes. Yet conductors hung on in Central London and on some major suburban corridors.

And, as we know, from the mid-1980s crew operation, using second-hand Routemasters, was reintroduced to many cities around Britain, in one of the most remarkable developments in the history of British public road transport. But it was an Indian Summer, not a lasting change of policy. Outside peak periods the economics simply didn't stack up. The world was moving on, and the two main roles of a conductor — collecting fares and controlling boarding and alighting of passengers — were changing beyond recognition.

The development of the Leyland Atlantean during the late 1950s had spelled the end of one of the conductor's duties, even if it wasn't fully realised at the time. With the driver controlling the doors and the doors controlling the passengers, boarding

Right: An early Leyland advertisement for the Atlantean highlights 'NO UNCOLLECTED FARES' and states: 'The enclosed front entrance, controlled by the driver, eliminates platform accidents … the conductor's sole job is fare collection'.

The Leyland 'ATLANTEAN'... → 78 SEATER

marks a HISTORIC ADVANCE in TRANSPORT DESIGN

The 'Atlantean' is the bus with everything! It is good for the operator because during peak hours it can accommodate more passengers than any other bus, but at off-peak times it costs no more to run than the normal double-decker. The enclosed front entrance, controlled by the driver, eliminates platform accidents ... the conductor's sole job is fare collection, while low platform, short stairways and wide gangways speed up loading and unloading.

For the passenger, there's controlled air-conditioning and ventilation, smooth riding (due to a remarkable new suspension system) and practically no noise or vibration. The driver comes off well, too! No engine noise in his cab ... the 125 h.p. diesel is mounted away at the back of the bus. Easier handling with Pneumo-cyclic gearbox and pedal control, lighter steering, greater stability and air-hydraulic braking system. Despite the increased passenger capacity, the 'Atlantean' is as manoeuvrable as a conventional double-decker and the low overall height of 13' 2¼" enables it to negotiate bridges. Full details of this remarkable bus are set out in our brochure 748 which be sent on application.

NO PLATFORM ACCIDENTS

NO UNCOLLECTED FARES

SAFEST TO OPERATE

LOWEST OVERALL HEIGHT

Above: Conductors did survive to work on some unlikely vehicles, such as this crew-operated Leyland National 2 operated by Paterson & Brown and seen on a local service in Beith, Ayrshire, in 1980. *Stewart J. Brown*

and alighting between authorised stops (and passengers swarming aboard already-overcrowded vehicles) ceased to be a problem, whilst the periscope mirror, however imperfect, gave the driver at least some idea of how full the top deck was. The mid-1960s move towards long single-deckers — and the sometimes-disastrous introduction of standee saloons — also undermined the conductor's job.

If front entrances and rear engines solved boarding-supervision problems, collecting fares — the other traditional task of the conductor — proved to be a much tougher nut to crack. In theory, placing some coins on a tray beside a driver whilst a ticket chattered out from a motorised Setright or TIM machine was easy. Or was it? Many passengers just could not (or would not) tender the correct fare.

Publicity campaigns, the tone of which alternated between the pleading, the threatening and the downright desperate, seemed to fall on deaf ears. Self-service machines just didn't work reliably enough. Turnstiles, where used, sometimes jammed, with helpless shoppers caught up in their gates. Most people tried to pay the harassed driver. Bus operators became ever more direct, one Glasgow poster screaming in broad Lowland Scots: "Pleez geezi right ferr …!". London Transport was more sniffy — "We're not impressed with big money".

Matters were made worse by repeated inflationary fare increases, sometimes more than one per year. Just as operators managed to coax crews and passengers into remembering the new fares, up they would go again, and it would be back to square one. Decimalisation in 1971 was another (albeit one-off) headache. But slowly, gradually, the concept of paying the driver without stopping the entire street took hold. Simplified fare structures, new technology and, most of all, pre-payment schemes such as Greater Manchester Transport's very successful SaverSeven travel pass and Clippercard multi-journey schemes, helped to reduce boarding times.

Fewer and fewer people paid cash or needed change. By 2004, although in the East Midlands some 56% of passengers still paid cash, this figure was down to 35% in the West Midlands, where the legendary Travelcard had been introduced in 1972. Most significantly of all, in London, brimming with lost tourists, it was down to just 23% — a fantastic achievement in uniquely difficult circumstances. Effectively, the need for conductors was arguably largely eliminated, even in London, and the final few hundred found themselves with plenty of tickets to check but few actual fares to collect. They were, of course, finally to bow out with the much-loved but ageing Routemasters.

But the conductor has not completely disappeared. You can still find them on many Blackpool trams. And the new Nottingham Express Transit uses conductors, complete with Wayfarer ticket machines, and is proud to do so. Perhaps, for these specialist operations, they've got it right. And maybe the conductor will make an occasional comeback, at least in a few 'one-off' circumstances. Nottingham's are certainly appreciated by the system's passengers, particularly when travelling at night.

The public generally resented the gradual change to one-person operation. Many now look back with nostalgia to a now-departed age, when conductors and conductresses called out stops, reminded passengers when to get off, rescued lost tourists and lost property, guided blind passengers to their seats and generally made things run smoothly. But that age is now over, and the accoutrements of the bus conductor — the Bell Punch, Setright or Gibson machine, the cash-bag, the peaked cap and the whistle on a chain — are now collectors' items and museum exhibits.

So let's remember the conductor and conductress with pride. All those "Any more fares please" calls, all those stairs, all those early starts in winter, those bleak bike-rides through wind and rain to be at the garage on time, those millions of cups of tea and canteen meals, and those long rides or walks home at dead of night. And many ex-conductors (and drivers) recall their work with great affection. Some now-closed garages, such as London Country's Chelsham, nowadays even have their own internet websites, listing all the staff that latterly worked there.

To those hundreds of thousands, or indeed now probably millions, who have trodden the saloon's floor-slats like actors on a moving stage, climbing that steep staircase countless times every hour, rattling loose change and giving information and advice, you did a good job, at all hours of the day and most hours of the night, and in all weathers. You got your passengers safely to their destinations (mostly) on time and always in one piece, and often with a friendly remark along the way. You were part of a way of life, in wartime and peacetime, depression and prosperity, and will always be remembered by the public with a very real affection.

Below: For bus users, one of the biggest drawbacks of the disappearance of conductors was the length of time it could take for a driver to collect fares. Passengers queue patiently in Perth in 1992, as the driver of a Stagecoach Olympian takes their money.
Stewart J. Brown

One Small Step...

GAVIN BOOTH looks at a decade of change in London, in which accessible buses have revolutionised the capital's fleet.

All photographs by Gavin Booth

The very first Ian Allan *ABC of London Transport Vehicles* that I bought new was the 15th edition, published in 1958. Its 80 pages painted a picture of a fleet that was so standardised, so efficiently organised …

And so-o-o-o boring.

There were 7,682 London Transport motorbuses listed, plus of course the still-massive 1,590-strong trolleybus fleet, giving a fleet total of over 9,000, but the motor-bus fleet consisted of barely 10 classes. The RT-type AEC Regent was a magnificent bus by any standards, but there were 4,460 of them — two-thirds of the double-deck total; add to them the not-dissimilar RTLs, on Leyland chassis, and the 500 wide Leyland RTWs, and the RT family totalled a staggering 98% of the LT double-deck fleet; the balance was made up of the 76 lowbridge AEC Regent IIIs of the RLH class and four new prototype buses called Routemasters. How different from today.

As readers will surely know, the RM was the last made-to-measure bus built for London service; everything since then has been adapted from proprietary types or has been designed by manufacturers with London orders in mind. Look at the largely unloved DMS-family Fleetlines, many of which enjoyed only short lives in London; or the Metrobuses and Titans, which, because they were designed with London orders in mind, actually enjoyed long lives in the Capital, clocking up 25 years from the first deliveries to the last withdrawals; and the present-day low-floor double-deck types, for which London is by far the biggest market.

As a frequent visitor to London I have observed the changes in the London bus fleet for more years than I care to admit, and to the visitor the changes are often more evident because you have that more detached involvement. It's like watching your children grow up: because you see them every day, you don't really notice it. But with other people's children, particularly grandchildren, you notice the differences much more.

The London fleet has been through many different phases since World War 2. There was the immediate postwar mix of prewar, utility and early postwar 'off-the-shelf' buses that allowed LT to struggle through until close on 7,000 members of the RT family came on stream. Then the Routemaster era in the 1960s, the unhappy Swift/Merlin and Fleetline years, the happier Metrobus and Titan years, the minibus years that led to the Dart years, the Olympian years, and now the low-floor years, with Transport for London guiding the operators towards an all-low-floor fleet by the end of 2005.

There surely hasn't been a time in the recent history of London's buses when the fleet has changed so much in a relatively short period — or, indeed, when the fleet has been so varied.

It all really started with privatisation. In 1994/5 what had latterly been the 11 subsidiaries of London Buses Ltd were sold off, raising more than £230 million. The main sales took place in a rush between September 1994 and January 1995 and involved nearly 5,000 buses and coaches. Four subsidiaries — CentreWest, London General, London United, and Metroline — went to management teams, Cowie Group bought Leaside and South London, Go-Ahead Group bought London Central, MTL Trust Holdings bought London Northern, and Stagecoach bought East London and Selkent. Earlier the small Stanwell Buses business, trading as Westlink, had been sold to its management.

The fleet that passed into new ownership was an interesting mixture. There were over 600 minibuses, dominated by two types, the MA-class Mercedes-Benz 811s with Alexander bodies and the MR- and MRL-class MCW Metroriders. There were nearly 800 midibuses, the vast majority Dennis Darts, and some 270 full-size single-deckers, including the rump of the LS-class Leyland Nationals, some converted as GLS-class Greenways, as well as Dennis Lances with Alexander, Northern Counties and Plaxton bodies, Volvo B10Bs with Northern Counties bodies and

Left: Currently under consideration for a light-rail project, express services on the Shepherd's Bush–Uxbridge corridor were in 1994 operated by Leyland Nationals, as here at Uxbridge station.

Below: Early deliveries of Dennis Darts to London had Duple Dartline bodies, like this 1990 London United example seen in Hounslow.

Bottom: The Dennis Dart with Reeve Burgess, later Plaxton, Pointer bodies quickly became a London standard. This 1993 London United example is seen crossing Richmond Bridge in 1999.

Above: Designed for London, the Leyland Titan B15 enjoyed a long innings in service in the capital. In the days before red buses became the rule a 1980-built Londonlinks Titan is seen in Trafalgar Square on the 176 in April 1995. Londonlinks was set up by British Bus to take over most of the LT contracts of London & Country.

Above: The MCW Metrobus vied with Leyland's Titan for London orders in the early 1980s. Those which were latterly operated by Metroline had a distinctive deep blue skirt. This 1985 bus was photographed at Victoria in 1999.

Left: A 1996 Volvo Olympian/Northern Counties Palatine from the London Central fleet crosses Waterloo Bridge on the 171.

Left: Stagecoach
inherited 42 1991/2-
built Scania N113DRB/
Northern Counties
Palatine I with the
East London business.
One is seen at Ilford
in 2001 with a First
Capital Dennis Arrow
in the background.

Right: For a time
very different liveries
could be enjoyed on
London's streets,
like this 1994 view
at Oxford Circus
with a 1991 London
& Country Volvo
Citybus/East Lancs
passing a London
United Routemaster.

those pioneering low-floor buses that heralded a massive change in the make-up of bus fleets throughout the UK. In 1994 London Buses had taken 68 Wright-bodied low floor single-deckers, 38 LLW-class Dennis Lance SLF and 30 SLW-class Scania N113CRL. Although London fleets would buy no more examples of these chassis, these deliveries paved the way for a massive revolution that would see low-floor buses sweep everything away over the next decade. Forty of these buses are among fewer than 500 buses from the 1995 list that survived into 2005.

The 1995 double-deck London fleet was dominated by the 1,425 remaining examples of the M-class MCW Metrobuses and the 785 T-class Leyland Titans. Even by 1995 the Routemaster

totals had dropped massively: there were just 141 RMs, 463 RMLs, 10 RMCs and three RMAs on the combined fleet strength. In addition there was the 263-strong Leyland Olympian/ECW L class, plus a host of newer Olympians with Leyland and Alexander bodywork. Other double-deck types represented included the rump of the DMS family of Fleetlines, two of the V-class Volvo Ailsas, 71 Scania N113DRB with Alexander and Northern Counties bodies, 39 Volvo B10M with Northern Counties bodies and the 25 fairly recent DAF DB250/Optare Spectras. All were what would soon become known as step-entrance double-deckers, to distinguish them from the low-floor double-deckers that would come on stream in London from 1998.

These were the 'red' London fleets, with their roots in London Transport. Following the introduction of route tendering in the 1980s there were other fleets providing LT services in 1995. Like Armchair, BTS, Capital Citybus, County Bus, Docklands Transit, Grey-Green, Kentish Bus, London Buslines, London & Country, Metrobus and Thamesway. The buses they used included the inevitable Mercedes-Benz minis, Darts and Olympians, plus some more unusual purchases — for instance, Capital Citybus and London & Country bought Dennis Dominators, and Kentish Bus and BTS operated Routemasters — and the buses were mostly painted in the operators' own liveries, which brought variety into Central London before the days of the 80%-red rule.

The ownership of several of these fleets would soon change, strengthening the London presence of the Cowie group in particular. Cowie's original presence in London had been through its Grey-Green fleet, and of course it had bought Leaside and South London in 1994. It subsequently bought County Bus and, with its purchase of British Bus, it also gained control of Kentish Bus and London & Country. Cowie later adopted the Arriva name. FirstGroup grew with the acquisition of both Capital Citybus and CentreWest (which had bought London Buslines), and Go-Ahead bought London General and Metrobus. More recently, London Sovereign (as BTS had become following takeover by Blazefield Holdings) passed to London United, and Armchair to Metroline.

Above: The Dennis Dart SLF/Plaxton Pointer quickly became London's favourite lowfloor model. Metroline and Sovereign Dennis Dart SLF/Plaxton Pointers are seen at Golders Green station in 2001. All are 10.1m examples. In 2002 Blazefield sold its Sovereign (London) business to London United.

Right: Dennis Darts with Caetano Nimbus bodies are not common in London. This 2001 10.5m example, in the Hackney Community Transport fleet for operation on the 153, is seen at Liverpool Street station.

Above: Comparatively rare in London service is the Optare Excel. This 10.7m-long bus is at the Lewisham Docklands Light Rail station in May 2003 in the fleet of East Thames Buses, which acquired it from Harris Bus.

Below: Bought for special services to the Millennium Dome at Greenwich, one of 17 DAF SB220 with East Lancs Myllennium bodies that are unique in the London bus fleet.

Right: Late-model Volvo Olympians for London operators included 44 with Alexander (Belfast) bodies bought in 1997/8. One operated by London United is seen at Surbiton station in 2002 on the busy 281 route.

Left: Unusual purchases by a London company were examples of the short-lived Dennis Arrow, built between 1996 and 1998, seen here at Ilford with East Lancs Pyoneer body, by which time their original operator, Capital Citybus, had become First Capital.

Right: Arriva's Alexander ALX400-bodied DAF DB250s were among London's earliest low-floor double-deckers. This 1999 10.2m-long example is seen at Brixton in 2003.

If the privatised companies created in 1995 inherited a fleet that reflected London Transport thinking, they soon started to stamp their individuality on their purchases. Of course there were continuing deliveries of Pointer Darts, and from 1996 these were increasingly of the low-floor SLF version — but not all; fleets like Metroline and Stagecoach took delivery of step-entrance Pointer Darts as late as 1997. The SLF Pointer Dart went on to become virtually the standard London single-decker, with deliveries to almost every operator. Some, like Armchair, Arriva and Stagecoach, favoured Alexander ALX200 bodies for some of their SLF Darts, while Marshall picked up useful orders for its Capital body from First's London fleets, London Central/General and Metroline. Rarer bodies on Dart SLF were the Caetano Nimbus (Limebourne), Wright Crusader (London United) and East Lancs Spryte (First Capital and Wings).

Although the Dart SLF accelerated the low-floor revolution in London, other low-floor single-deckers included Optare Excels delivered to Harris Bus, London United, Metrobus, Thorpe's and Travel London, Volvo B6BLE/Sprytes for London Traveller, and Optare Solos for Travel London. New full-size low-floor single-deckers were rare in the London fleets, but London General took 17 DAF SB220/East Lancs Myllennium for services to the Millennium Dome, and Tellings-Golden Miller bought Volvo B10BLE/Alexander ALX300s for the peripheral 726 express service.

Low-floor double-deckers were slow to materialise. DAF won the race to introduce them to the streets of London, in 1998, with DB250 deliveries to Arriva, but Dennis was close behind with its Trident; Volvo had lost some time when it had to redesign its original low-floor double-deck offering, finally coming up with the B7TL in 1999. Before the Trident there had been a new step-entrance double-decker from Dennis, the Arrow, bought in the years 1996-8 by Capital Citybus and subsequently transferred to First's provincial fleets — an example of a type that did not exist in 1995 yet had disappeared from London within the decade.

Once the manufacturers had got into their stride with low-floor double-deckers there was no stopping them. In the first two years that they were available — 1999 and 2000 — more than 1,000 were bought for London service; each year more of these buses took to the streets, and the peak came in 2003,

Below: First London standardised largely on Plaxton President bodywork for its early low-floor double-deckers, but in 2003 it bought 28 TransBus ALX400-bodied 10.6m Volvo B7TLs, like this one in Oxford Street in 2003.

Right: A 1999 Metroline Dennis Trident/Plaxton President pulls out of London Bridge station in 2000.

Left: One of 23 9.9m TransBus Trident/ Presidents bought by London Central in 2003 passes Westminster Abbey when new.

Right: The stylish Wright Eclipse Gemini body has been specified by a number of London fleets. This London General Volvo B7TL is seen at Piccadilly Circus when new in 2002.

Above: Metrobus introduced a new type to London service with the Scania N94/East Lancs OmniDekka, as here at Croydon when new in 2003.

when more than 1,000 low-floor double-deckers entered service with London operators. This was, of course, the year when Congestion Charging was introduced in London, and part of the Mayor's strategy was a package of public-transport improvements, including brand-new bus routes.

With three manufacturers — DAF, Dennis and Volvo — supplying chassis and initially four builders — Alexander, East Lancs, Optare and Plaxton — supplying bodies, there was capacity to meet the artificially high demand for low-floor double-deckers triggered by Mayor Ken Livingstone's promise that all London bus routes would be accessible by the end of 2005. Two more suppliers came on to the scene later — Scania, which has yet to make a big impact on the London market, and Wright, which since 2001 has built some 600 of its striking Gemini body for London customers.

The operating companies had their favoured suppliers, but only Stagecoach stuck to one chassis/body combination, while the others resisted the temptation to put all their eggs in one manufacturer's basket. The Stagecoach choice was the Dennis Trident with Alexander ALX400 body, initially in 10.5m-long, low-height form but soon with normal-height bodies, in both 10.5m and 9.9m lengths.

The other operators have spread their favours more widely. Arriva has bought DAF DB250s and Volvo B7TLs but has resisted the lure of the Dennis Trident. First, Go-Ahead, London United and Metroline have dual-sourced, taking Tridents and B7TLs; London United and Go-Ahead's Metrobus fleet have additionally bought Scania N94s. The smaller companies have tended to stick to one supplier, Tridents going to Armchair, Blue Triangle and Hackney Community Transport and B7TLs to East Thames and Travel London.

Similarly, Alexander and Plaxton were the favoured bodybuilders for Arriva, First, Go-Ahead, London United and Metroline — at least until Wright came along with bodies (on the DB250 and B7TL) which attracted all of these except Metroline to buy some. East Lancs has made a lesser impact on the London scene, but of the 'big' fleets Go-Ahead and London United have bought Vyking bodies as well as OmniDekkas on their Scania N94s.

The double-decker is still seen as the archetypal London bus and still accounts for more than 60% of the fleet. But the double-deck's future role in London was put in doubt with the introduction in 2002 of articulated single-deckers, initially for Go-Ahead's Red Arrow services, but from 2003 on routes that paralleled sections of existing double-deck routes. The Mercedes-Benz Citaro was the choice, following experiments with Volvo B7LA/Wright artics borrowed from provincial First fleets on the 207 service between Shepherd's Bush and Hayes. By the end of 2004 there were 279

Right: The Mercedes-Benz Citaro G introduced articulated-bus operation on a regular basis in London. This 2003 Stagecoach example is seen turning into Parliament Square on the 453 when new.

Left: A once-common sight at London termini, a gaggle of Routemasters lay over at Putney Heath, terminus of the 14, due to be one of the last routes operated by this iconic type.

Right: The famous 11 route was still Routemaster-operated in 2003, when this London General RML was seen at the Bank.

Citaro artics in service, spread between the Arriva, First, Go-Ahead and Stagecoach fleets, and both Scania and Volvo have provided artic demonstrators to try to break the Citaro's dominance of the market.

The artics introduced to London's streets the concept of cashless buses. Passengers could not pay the driver and had to have a valid ticket; single-journey and day tickets were sold from machines at bus stops.

The arrival of the artics caused some consternation among passengers and enthusiasts who were concerned that these were being put forward as an alternative to double-deckers, including their beloved Routemasters. In 2004 fires destroyed three of the Citaro artics and severely damaged a fourth, but Mercedes-Benz responded quickly to rectify the situation, and the artic looks set to play a small but very visible part on the London bus scene.

If all goes to plan, the London 'red bus' fleet will be entirely low-floor by the end of 2005, which heralds the end of the Routemaster and the remaining step-entrance single- and double-deckers. While the Darts and Olympians may not be missed and will quickly find homes outside London, many regret the passing of the Routemaster, for so long a symbol of London. The reality is that many of the remaining buses are looking and sounding as if they are past their sell-by date, and the promise of an RM-operated heritage route in Central London should mean that they won't disappear completely.

No doubt the low-floor types that have been entering service in London over the past few years

will continue to figure in the orders from the London operators. Following the collapse of TransBus and the creation of Alexander Dennis the President body is no longer available, but we are promised the Enviro400 double-decker, which will offer a better low-floor arrangement, while the Enviro200 single-decker, designed with London in mind, is likely to start appearing on the capital's streets. MAN has joined the ranks of European manufacturers offering a double-deck model in the UK, and Optare has long been developing a side-engined double-decker, again with London in mind. These new models may have missed the boat in terms of bulk double-deck orders from London operators — the composition and relative youth of the London double-deck fleet may mean that there will be fewer orders for a year or two — but it could be that the big groups cascade their earlier low-floor 'deckers to their other UK fleets (as Stagecoach has done) and buy new buses for London.

Today's London fleet may be less standardised than it was in the days of the RT family, and arguably a bit less quirky without Routemasters, but in terms of accessibility London has led the way. There are a few smaller operators around the UK that can boast 100%-accessible fleets, but TfL and the London operators will have created an 8,000-bus low floor fleet in barely a decade, and that, by any measure, is a tremendous achievement.

I Was Responsible

All photographs by the author

Over a 40-year career in the bus industry ROY MARSHALL was responsible for a wide range of decisions. He looks back on some of the more interesting, including some which were not quite what he had planned.

During World War 2 I travelled across Nottingham to school, which increased my interest in buses and encouraged my desire to move into the business. Wherever I travelled I made notes of different types of vehicles in a fleet, to enable me to produce drawings. My choice of a job would have been to become a draughtsman at Nottingham City Transport, but by the time I left school in 1946 the choice of jobs was restricted, as men being discharged from the armed forces had a guarantee of returning to their previous jobs.

While I was visiting operators to obtain fleet details Arthur Skill had told me that he would give me employment when I left school, so I took up his offer. At that time there was a great demand for coach trips — excursions, private hires and, in the summer, for the express service to Bridlington and Scarborough. New vehicles were on order, and the varied fleet of prewar vehicles was in urgent need of reconditioning, especially bodywork. All sorts of firms entered the coach-repair market, as most local operators were in a similar position.

I was allowed to specify certain bodywork aspects of new vehicles, introduce my ideas of fleet numbering and visit firms where coachwork was being rebuilt or reconditioned. It was a wonderful start to my career. Today, however, would people be willing to work a 5½- or six-day week with one week's holiday (plus bank holidays) for £2.10 a week — or its current value adjusted for inflation?

In the summer period I helped supervise the loading of coaches to the coast, travelled to Bridlington, then helped to load them for their return. One Saturday I made the dreadful mistake of omitting 100 from the number of passengers waiting at a road junction about 20 miles north of Nottingham and looking forward to their week's holiday at the coast. The error had been discovered by a senior driver on the last coach, whose job was to pick up the last passengers and ensure the operation ran smoothly. A call to base meant that three coaches and drivers had to be found immediately, and somehow they managed it. Fortunately, apart from a few grumbles no

Left: This 1942 Tilling-Stevens in the Skills fleet had a chassis built for Hong Kong. It had a 30-seat Willowbrook body and was once used for a journey on the Bridlington express service, along with a van filled with luggage. It would go up hill and down dale in top gear, its driver carrying a brick to place on the accelerator!

Right: The modernisation of the body on this Skills Guy Arab was the author's responsibility. It was one of three used on both regular and works services.

Left: The author was responsible for the interior finish, the twin destination indicators, the matching fleet and registration numbers and the aluminium side mouldings on the Duple bodies on a batch of Skills Daimler CVD6s. Three were ordered, but two were diverted to Gash of Newark because of a reduction in work.

Right: Skills' first underfloor-engined coaches, in 1951, were a Leyland Royal Tiger and an AEC Regal IV. This is the Regal IV, with Harrington body. The twin front destination displays allowed the coach to display information such as 'Express Service' and 'Scarborough'. The queue in this 1954 view is for the Newton Air Display.

complaints were received, but I was hauled in front of the boss and his son.

In 1951 Nottingham City Transport was advertising vacancies, and I successfully applied for a job in the traffic office. My role was to deal with contract hire, take telephone calls of complaint and arrange disciplinary interviews. Later I received training in the mileage and traffic-timekeeping offices and was transferred to the important schedules office, but not before I had made another mistake — of cancelling the wrong late-night-dance specials ordered by a hospital-management committee; it transpired that two hospital-management committees had ordered buses, but on different dates. Fortunately such buses were driven by night-shift drivers/cleaners, so the

required buses were soon on the way. I was sent to apologise to the organiser.

My positive contributions to the 'I was responsible' theme included simplifying office systems. In my job of arranging contract hires there was often a need to display a route number and 'Special', but only the oldest buses in the fleet could display separate route numbers, as all new vehicles had single blinds. I drew this to the attention of the section head (as, no doubt, did others), and eventually the policy was changed and future new buses had separate route-number boxes.

After a bout of ill health and time off work in 1954/5 I passed my Institute of Transport examinations and joined the schedules office, but after a while I decided the time was right to move on.

Left: In a conversation at Huntingdon Street bus station in Nottingham Alan Gash asked Roy Marshall where he could get some double-deckers quickly for improved services between Nottingham and Newark. Roy directed him to Wigan Corporation, which had just sold some TD1 Titans to Barton Transport, and two Wigan Titans duly joined the Gash fleet in July 1947.

Right: Two vehicles numbered 9 in the Nottingham City Transport fleet in 1958. The AEC Regent on the left is 20 years old and has a Metro-Cammell body. Its replacement, a Leyland Titan PD2/40, also has a Metro-Cammell body. The interiors of the bodies had flush windows, the theory being that the exterior could be washed efficiently by a washing machine while the flush interior finish would save time on hand-cleaning.

Southport

In the autumn of 1958 I moved to Southport Corporation as traffic superintendent, responsible to the General Manager, Jackson Hoggard. His father was the retired manager of Chesterfield Corporation Transport, where he had used his influence for Jackson to spend some time in the traffic section at Nottingham. It was therefore quite satisfying that the Southport system incorporated many working practices with which I was familiar. For example, drivers were paid a signing-on and signing-off allowance when taking a bus out or returning one to the depot, but when they were relieved in the town centre their pay stopped at that time.

I returned from a short holiday in the spring of 1959 to find open-top double-deckers running a seasonal service from Ainsdale Beach via the town to Botanic Gardens. The crews were on overtime, and the buses were carrying fresh air — no wonder losses were being incurred! "We do this every year," came the response when I queried the operation. The route was changed to operate as far as possible as a circular and was then advertised as a circular tour, operating at times when visitors were around. Subsequently economies were made by restricting the enhanced summer timetable to the period of the school holidays. Later still, experiments were carried out with one-man operation, as I saw this as a way to make further savings and to retain staff through better pay.

Economies were also made by more efficient scheduling and by employing standby staff during

Right: Southport was essentially a Leyland operator, apart from wartime Daimlers and some AECs and Crossleys delivered in 1949. By 1958 the Regent IIIs had become unpopular because of heavy steering and were only used at peak periods.

Left: Easter usually found the worst traffic congestion in Southport, as this was the only Bank Holiday, apart from Christmas, to be observed by all towns in the North West of England. This played havoc with Southport Corporation's bus services, most of which were cross-town. The author arranged for services to turn short of the town centre, which practice required more vehicles but ensured that they ran on time. This 1963 view depicts three Titans in King Street, terminus for southbound services. Both Roy Marshall and the fleet's engineer wanted to introduce Leyland Atlanteans, but they were over-ruled by the General Manager, who was influenced by reports of poor operational experiences with early Atlanteans at Ribble.

Right: Southport used Lincoln Tiger Cubs, a Manchester Panther Cub and a Kingston-upon-Hull Panther on experimental one-man operation on its least-used services. The Lincoln and Hull vehicles had not been used as one-man buses in their home cities because of union opposition, but there was no such problem at Southport. This view dates from 1965.

Left: There were 12 Tiger PS1s and AEC Regal IIIs at Gelligaer which had to be replaced by larger vehicles. The highest offer received for this Longwell Green-bodied Regal when it was withdrawn was £25, which prompted Roy Marshall to adopt a policy of writing to operators he thought might be interested in buying withdrawn buses, inviting them to submit sealed bids for consideration by the Transport Committee Chairman.

Right: Increased capacity was created in the Gelligaer fleet by buying two AEC Reliances from Jones of Aberbeeg. This one had an unusual metal-framed Duple Midland body with one curved windscreen.

Right: For trunk services to Newport Roy Marshall ordered three Bristol VRTs, chosen because their gearbox and axle ratios were best suited to the fast, flat sections of the route while being able to cope with steep hills out of Newport and Bargoed. They had Northern Counties bodies and were finished in the prewar livery of red, white and green.

the times when they were most likely to be used. Thus it was possible to have one less standby driver and conductor, except early on Friday mornings — because Thursday was pay-day, which meant late nights out, with more staff failing to turn out for Friday's early shifts.

The various changes which I introduced, together with radical changes made on the engineering side by a new engineer who took advantage of the reliability of Leyland O.600 engines and metal-framed bodies, resulted in a profit being recorded during the winter months — the first time for many years. This enabled an extension to Canning Road depot to be funded out of reserves and the Hesketh Road depot to be closed.

I thoroughly enjoyed my time at Southport, which was a wonderful place to work (and live), helped by a co operative union secretary and a boss who allowed his heads of departments to get on with the job their own way as long as they kept him informed. However, if I was to further my career it was time to move on once again.

Gelligaer

My successful application was to Gelligaer Urban District Council for the post of omnibus manager with a fleet of 30 buses. These were numbered 1–30, and I duly renumbered them in order of age instead of the previous gap-filling system, which I detested from my younger days when trying to compile a Midland General fleet list.

What a fascinating area it was: colliery villages and a town, Bargoed. There were steep-sided valleys and what was claimed to be the tallest slagheap in Britain, and ponies that sheltered in bus shelters and tipped over dustbins looking for food. At the time of my appointment there was

no one on the staff who could compile duty schedules from scratch. And there was no preventive maintenance. Buses were inspected by the Ministry of Transport, with many defects being found and then rectified. The painter simply touched up panels, as a bus could not be spared long enough for repainting. However, after he retired, when buses could be made available they were spray-painted by the coachbuilder.

The Bellgraphic ticket system was still in use. This required two machines per duty, plus two more for the next day (plus others for a weekend), and needed one person full-time to deal with tickets. When he retired I recommended the replacement of the Bellgraphics by second-hand Setright machines, which I knew had just been displaced at MacBraynes. I did, however, find that new conductors had a good idea of how much they should be paying in and pocketed most of the 'overs' — more than I had budgeted for. South Wales was notorious for the practice of conductors taking half the fare and allowing the passenger to keep half, with no ticket issued.

Another local custom was, in general, for crews to take out the popular buses, which usually led to 35-seat half-cabs' being left for school runs, which actually needed high-capacity AEC Reliances. All this changed when two second-hand and two new Reliances were bought, together with two ex-demonstrators — a Swift and a Panther — which I knew to be standing idle at their manufacturers' premises.

Burton-upon-Trent

In 1971 I made a further move, this time to Burton-upon-Trent, in order to be nearer to my father following the death of my mother.

Left: Troublesome constant-mesh gearboxes led to the premature withdrawal of Burton's Daimler CSG5s. They had Massey bodies.

Below: The Burton fleet included a number of Willowbrook-bodied Fleetline saloons. These were available for conversion to one-man operation, but their length made them less manœuvrable than other types.

Left: The Civic Society in Burton felt that the town's maroon bus fleet looked drab, so Roy Marshall adopted Gelligaer's red, white and green colours, as seen on this Willowbrook-bodied Fleetline.

Above: In 1971, aware that Marshall-bodied Leyland Panthers built for Stratford Blue were lying unused at Midland Red, the author drew this to the attention of Preston Transport, which duly bought them.

Left: ... And four years later he was instrumental in finding new homes for Panthers redundant at West Yorkshire PTE, alerting the manager of Chesterfield Transport, a Panther user, to their availability.

Surprisingly the trade union had been requesting one-man operation, but no plans had been made and few vehicles were suitable. But 12 Daimler Fleetline double-deckers were awaited, orders having been placed for delivery over four years. To help inaugurate one-man operation two Leyland Royal Tigers and two Tiger Cubs were bought from Bournemouth Corporation.

Burton still increased service frequencies at lunchtime, these covering the old-established daytime peak when workers went home for lunch. Following the delivery of new buses a start was made on withdrawing the older Daimlers, the first being CSG5s which had troublesome gearboxes but excellent Massey bodies. Disposals were made

by picking out possible purchasers and writing to them. This resulted in all being sold, one purchaser being McLennan of Spittalfield.

One of my clearest memories of Burton is of the former tram depot, which became full of diesel fumes and smoke when Gardner 5LW engines were started up prior to the morning run-out.

In 1974 Burton was united with other authorities to become East Staffordshire District Council, and my post was made responsible to the Borough Engineer. To me this was unnecessary and wasteful, so I applied for jobs elsewhere, there being a number of managerial posts available as a result of other local-authority amalgamations at that time.

Burnley & Pendle

In 1974 I became General Manager of the newly formed Burnley & Pendle Joint Committee, which had replaced that of Burnley, Colne & Nelson, formed in 1933. I was surprised to find that, even after all these years, the platform staff were still represented by three different branches of the same trade union. The Nelson operatives, having had their local depot closed, collected buses from Burnley but were controlled by an inspector at Nelson bus station. Colne depot was still open and at that time was useful in recruiting staff in that area. However, only routine maintenance was undertaken there, all other work, including administration, being conducted by the Burnley offices and workshops, the latter producing some first-class work. Eventually the separate union branches were amalgamated.

BCN had been a pioneer in one-man operation, using Tiger Cubs, earlier Tiger PS1s and PS2s (which had been converted from rear- to forward-entrance) and finally a batch of Panthers. Titan PD3s were in the process of being sold, but many forward-entrance PD2s were in use, whilst Leopard coaches had recently been introduced, together with Bristol REs, Seddon RUs and Leyland Nationals.

BCN policy in recent years had been to purchase only single-deckers. One route was said not to be a candidate for one-man operation, but after a few months at Burnley & Pendle I came to the conclusion that it should be converted, using double-deckers. The order went to Bristol and East Lancs, as Leyland told me at that time that only

VRTs and Titans were available! Subsequently Leyland had to change this policy and retain the Atlantean. The Bristol VRT double-deckers replaced the PS2 buses, many of which were purchased for preservation.

The Gardner-engined REs proved to be excellent machines, but when more were required Leyland said that it could supply only Nationals — which still had teething troubles but excellent body shells. Further bus orders were therefore for the reliable Leopard PSU4 with East Lancs bodywork, until the National 2 was introduced. The Seddons had certain problems which could have been ironed out with further development — and Burnley & Pendle was one of the operators which met with Seddon's representatives to request this — but it came to nothing when Seddon was sold to new owners with no interest in developing the RU.

Second-hand REs and Nationals were bought to replace the Seddons, both types coming from Tyne & Wear PTE. Our contact at the PTE for the purchase of these vehicles was one Moir Lockhead, who three decades later would be Chief Executive of Britain's biggest transport group, First.

With the approach of deregulation in 1986 I decided to retire, and did so that summer, having completed 40 years in the bus industry.

Below: At Burnley & Pendle the author adopted what had been East Midland Motor Services livery — orange, cream and brown — for coaches, including two Duple-bodied Leopards used on the service from Colne to London.

Above: The first second-hand single-deckers for Burnley & Pendle were former Sunderland Corporation Bristol RELLs with Metro-Cammell bodies, purchased from Tyne & Wear PTE.

Below: Tayside Transport provided some Bristol VRTs for Burnley & Pendle, and these proved invaluable for certain school workings. They entered service in Tayside blue but were soon repainted in Burnley & Pendle livery and rebuilt to single-door layout. Burnley & Pendle was going to take new Alexander-bodied VRTs but switched the body order to ECW when late delivery from Alexander threatened the loss of New Bus Grant funding.

Changing Times in Scotland

As the last vehicles purchased by the Scottish Bus Group slowly vanish, STEWART J. BROWN looks back over the last two decades and examines the varied fates of Scotland's public-sector bus operators.

All photographs by the author

Loads of buses, loads of operators. These weren't quite the words used by the Conservative Government when it set about reforming the bus industry in the 1980s, but that was its aim with its twin policies of privatisation and deregulation.

And, for a short period, it happened. In the late 1980s there was a proliferation of new bus operators, or new owners for established businesses.

Then, in the early 1990s the industry gradually coalesced, creating new groups, with new territories.

In Scotland, prior to the upheaval of the mid-1980s, the vast majority of bus services were run by public-sector businesses. Independents played but a small part, most noticeably in Paisley, Lanarkshire, the Ayrshire coast and parts of the Highlands.

So most bus users travelled on vehicles owned by one of seven Scottish Bus Group companies, three municipal fleets or the one Passenger Transport Executive, which between them ran most of the country's bus services with a fleet of around 5,000 vehicles. The number of SBG subsidiaries increased to 11 in 1985 and was then reduced to nine in 1989 as the Group struggled to compete profitably in Glasgow and west central Scotland.

Twenty years on, most of the fleets which once made up Scotland's public sector bus operations are owned by four of the big UK groups — Stagecoach, First, Arriva and National Express. Yorkshire Traction also owns one former SBG business, Strathtay, while another, Highland, is independently owned. There is one fleet still in local-authority ownership — Lothian Buses. The other two, Grampian and Tayside, are part of First and National Express respectively. Between them

these operators run some 4,000 vehicles — a 20% reduction on the equivalent mid-1980s figure.

To some extent this reduction has been offset by growth in the number of small operators, although of the really well-known names of the 1980s it could be argued that only one — Hutchison of Overtown — survives two decades on. Most of the small operators serving Scotland in the early years of the 21st century are comparatively young post-deregulation companies.

Glasgow is the only Scottish city where all three of the big bus groups have a presence.

In the city and most of the surrounding area, First is the major operator. First Glasgow embraces the former Strathclyde PTE bus operation, along with all of what was Central Scottish, plus the southern operations of Midland Scottish, which from 1985 were part of the short-lived Kelvin Scottish company. When SBG was forced to retrench in 1989 Kelvin was amalgamated with Central to create a new Kelvin Central Buses business. This was bought in 1994 by Strathclyde Buses, which in turn was bought by FirstBus in 1996.

Also serving Glasgow is Stagecoach, primarily through its Western Buses business. This is the former Western Scottish company, which was bought by its management in 1991 and then resold to Stagecoach three years later. Western Buses operates to the southwest of Glasgow — it is the major operator in Ayrshire and Dumfries — and in Glasgow itself also operates as Magic Bus.

The third of the big groups to have a share of the action in Glasgow is Arriva's only Scottish business. This is Arriva Scotland West, the former Clydeside Scottish operation to the west of Glasgow. Clydeside was created in 1985 by the splitting of Western Scottish and was briefly reunited with Western in 1989 before being separated again in

Left: The sound of
Ailsas could still be
heard in Glasgow in
2005, although with
a major investment
programme by First
it is unlikely any will
survive into 2006.

Right: Although built
to the new standard
FirstBus specification,
the first Volvo
Olympians with
Alexander Royale
bodies for operation
in Glasgow were
delivered in all-over
red. The Greater
Glasgow fleetname
was short-lived.

1991 as part of a deal struck when Western was privatised. It was bought by Arriva predecessor British Bus in 1994.

Each of the groups has its own approach to vehicle policy. First Glasgow inherited what can most kindly be described as a varied selection of vehicles from its constituents, and some 20-year-old veterans survived in frontline service in 2005. However, their days were clearly numbered, as during the year the company introduced the biggest concentrated investment in new buses that the fleet had seen for many years, starting at the end of 2004 with the first of 84 Wrightbus Eclipse Gemini-bodied Volvo double-deckers. Indeed, Wrightbus products dominate the city, with both the current Eclipse on Volvo B7L chassis and the earlier Renown and Axcess-Ultralow models on Volvo B10BLE and Scania L94 respectively.

The veterans on their way out included unusual Gardner-engined Leyland Tigers with Alexander TS-type bodies and front-engined Ailsas with Alexander R-type bodies. Other older types include Volvo B10Ms with Alexander PS bodies — a type bought in large numbers by Kelvin Central in the mid 1990s. The reliable mid-engined Volvo B10M seemed like a good buy at the time — as indeed it was — but it meant that Kelvin Central was buying significant numbers of step-entrance buses at a time when forward-looking operators were starting to buy low-floor models. Alongside, say, a Dennis Dart SLF/Plaxton Pointer of the same age, a P registered B10M/PS looks distinctly like a bus from another era. Which, of course, it is.

For a long period there were relatively few new double-deckers for First Glasgow. There were numbers of Olympians, including long-wheelbase

Right: The Kelvin name was carried briefly by some FirstBus vehicles, including this unusual East Lancs-bodied Scania K93, seen arriving in Glasgow from Cumbernauld. It was one of three delivered in 1993.

Left: New in Greater Glasgow red, a batch of Volvo Olympians with Northern Counties Palatine II bodies was soon repainted in corporate First colours. One loads in St Enoch bus station.

Below: The Alexander ALX300 is not a common type in First ownership. A fleet of 30 on Volvo B10BLE chassis was delivered to Glasgow in 2000, but they were soon transferred to Aberdeen. One is seen when new at Clydebank.

Above: **Stagecoach operates Magic Bus services in Glasgow, most of the vehicles being Alexander-bodied Olympians transferred from Busways in Newcastle.**

models with Alexander Royale bodies which were delivered in 1996/7 in the company's then drab livery of unrelieved red but were soon repainted in corporate 'Barbie' style … and were then transferred to First Edinburgh. Then, in 2002, came the most unusual double-deckers in the fleet — possibly in the country — in the shape of 10 Volvo B7Ls with Copenhagen-style East Lancs Nordic bodies. These have three axles, 95 seats, are 12m long and just 4.1m high, and even feature air-conditioning.

Double-deck numbers were kept up by transferring vehicles in from other First fleets, the most interesting being 21 Dennis Dominators with dual-door Northern Counties bodies, which came from London. New in 1990, they were moved north in 2003. They are the only Dominators in service with a major-group company in Scotland — although in the early 1980s the Dominator was the standard Central Scottish double-decker and was therefore a common sight in Glasgow.

First runs articulated Wrightbus-bodied Volvos in the city, and Stagecoach runs articulated Volvo coaches on some of its express services, making Glasgow one of the few places outside London where you can see articulated vehicles operated by two different fleets.

Most of Stagecoach's out-of-town services are operated by conventional 12m Volvo B10M coaches, usually with Plaxton Premiere bodies, but on some services coach-seated double-deckers are used, most notably Volvo Citybuses running in to Glasgow from Fife. Double-deck coaches of a different type, Neoplan Skyliners, were introduced to Stagecoach's Megabus services from Glasgow in 2005.

Sharing the Megabus dark-blue livery is Magic Bus, and most of the vehicles providing Magic Bus services in Glasgow are elderly, including Alexander-bodied buses from Busways in Newcastle. Incidentally, the term 'elderly' in relation to buses usually carries the implication of vehicles which are a bit tired and uncared for — but that's not the case with Stagecoach, whose low-cost Magic Bus vehicles are turned out to the same high standard as the rest of the fleet and often put to shame more modern buses run by a certain other operator in the city …

Arriva's Scottish operations have not always seen the same levels of investment as have been put into the group's businesses in England and Wales. For example, there are no modern double-deckers in the fleet — indeed none bought new by Arriva Scotland West or any of its predecessors. The most modern are Volvo Citybuses with Alexander R type bodies, which were new to Grey Green in London. Other ex-London types to have seen service with Arriva Scotland West have included MCW Metrobuses, primarily for school contracts, and

former GreyGreen Volvo B10M single-deckers.

Arriva's single-deck fleet in Scotland is more modern, and the company was an early user of low-floor buses back in 1995, when Clydeside, as it then was, bought a number of stock Scanias as part of an urgent fleet modernisation by its new owners, British Bus. These just happened to include some low-floor vehicles, rather than being part of a thought-out policy, and were an odd mixture of step-entrance models bodied by Alexander, East Lancs and Northern Counties and low-floor East Lancs-bodied buses. They helped replace a large fleet of Leyland Leopards with Alexander Y-type bodies, some of which survived to see service in the 21st century, although none received Arriva corporate livery.

British Bus did then invest in new low-floor buses for Clydeside, taking Dennis Dart SLFs with both Plaxton Pointer and Alexander ALX200 bodies. Arriva Scotland West has, arguably, the most contested territory in Scotland, and over the years two of its major centres of operation — Paisley and Greenock — have been served by large numbers of low-cost (and often short-lived) minibus operators. In the end Arriva gave up in Greenock, a town

which in the heyday of the Scottish Bus Group was home to a Western SMT garage housing 150 vehicles.

Over to the east, Edinburgh's major bus operator, Lothian Buses, has survived the vicissitudes of deregulation despite attacks from Eastern Scottish in the late 1980s and from First Edinburgh at the start of the 21st century.

Out-of-town services are in the main provided by First Edinburgh, which is the successor to Eastern Scottish and also to Lowland Scottish, which from 1985 provided services in the Borders area. Both Eastern and Lowland were bought by GRT Holdings, one of the predecessors of First, in 1994.

Over the years Lothian and its predecessor, Edinburgh City Transport, gained a reputation for the high-quality appearance of their fleet — and that is one thing which hasn't changed.

After years of buying Alexander-bodied Leyland Atlanteans and Olympians, and then Volvo versions of the Olympian, Lothian abandoned its two major suppliers when it switched to low-floor models in 1999. Out went Alexander, and in came Plaxton, with the President. And out went Volvo, and in came Dennis, with the Trident.

There are now 197 Tridents running for Lothian Buses (including five with Alexander ALX400 bodywork), although whether or not there will be any more is an open question. There will clearly be no more Presidents, as the TransBus Wigan factory

Left: Arriva's double-deckers in Scotland are all second-hand. This Alexander-bodied Volvo Citybus was new to London operator Grey-Green. It is seen in Pollok in 2000.

Right: Clydeside had a large fleet of Leyland Leopards with Alexander Y-type bodies. Most had been new to Western SMT, but this one was a former Lancaster City Transport bus. It is seen in Greenock, a town no longer served by Arriva, Clydeside's successor.

Left: GRT transferred Leyland Atlanteans from its Grampian operation to other Scottish fleets, generally to replace Daimler Fleetlines. GRT used a standardised livery layout but with colours which reflected the heritage of the company — in this case green and yellow, the colours used by Lowland. The FirstBus logo reveals this to be a post-1996 view in Galashiels. The Atlantean has an Alexander body.

Left: The old order at Lothian — an Alexander-bodied Leyland Olympian, new in 1989, still looking smart in Princes Street in 2004.

Below: And the new — a TransBus-built Trident delivered in 2004 and bearing a registration recalling much earlier generations of Edinburgh bus.

Right: In the early days of FirstBus a strange variety of vehicles carried the group's '*f*' logo, such as this Alexander-bodied Ailsa operated by SMT before the creation of First Edinburgh.

Left: Edinburgh is one of the few places in Britain where Alexander Royales can be seen in service with two different operators. A 1997 Lothian Volvo Olympian leads a First Edinburgh example dating from 1998.

Right: Operated by Stagecoach between Fife and Edinburgh is a fleet of Mercedes-Benz taxibuses. This one, being watched by a startled kangaroo on the back of a Lothian Olympian, is empty.

has closed, and in 2005 Lothian took delivery of 50 Volvo B7TLs with Wrightbus Eclipse Gemini bodies.

The company has built up a large fleet of Super Pointer Darts, but its newest single-deckers feature stylish Wrightbus Eclipse bodies on Volvo's B7RLE chassis. Lothian Buses has also been running a Scania/East Lancs OmniDekka demonstrator on long-term evaluation and was the first operator to order Scania's new OmniCity double-decker, taking five in 2005.

While First Edinburgh has not enjoyed the levels of investment in new vehicles made by Lothian, it does run modern buses, including Scania/ Wrightbus Solars and Volvo Olympians with Alexander Royale bodies. But in recent years the overwhelming impression has been of tired, older, buses, ranging from Leyland Olympians and Ailsas inherited from SBG to mid-1990s Wright-bodied Scanias bought in the days of GRT. These types, which did not meet the criteria initially adopted for FirstBus's 'willow-leaf' livery, were briefly painted in

Above: The Gardner-engined Tigers bought by the Scottish Bus Group in the mid-1980s have proved remarkably durable buses, with many still in service in 2005. Most retain the drab overall red used by First Glasgow before the introduction of the so-called 'Barbie 2' corporate colour scheme. This is Hamilton bus station.

Below left: Originally in Tayside livery, this East Lancs-bodied Scania was Scotland's first low floor bus, in 1993. Fittingly Travel Dundee became the first major urban bus operator in Britain to provide 100% low-floor services, in 2004.

a scheme featuring stripes of green, yellow and blue on a cream base.

Stagecoach also runs into Edinburgh, primarily on services from Fife, including those operated by yellow-liveried and poorly patronised taxibuses. The expanding Megabus express-service network connects Edinburgh with London, Glasgow and cities to the north, including Perth and Aberdeen. In 2004 Stagecoach took over the M8 Motorvator service, which competed with Scottish Citylink on the Edinburgh–Glasgow corridor, and replaced the ageing Van Hool-bodied Volvos on the service with double-deck Jonckheere-bodied MAN coaches displaced from the Oxford Tube by new Neoplans.

Between Edinburgh and Glasgow First is the only substantial bus operator. In Lanarkshire it's First Glasgow; in Stirlingshire it's First Edinburgh, whose operations quaintly extend northwest of Glasgow to embrace the former Midland Scottish depot at Balfron.

The red livery used by First Glasgow is slowly disappearing from the region but at the start of

Above: In Yorkshire Traction ownership Strathtay retained its unusual orange, blue and white livery. Among early purchases after privatisation was this Dennis Dart with Northern Counties body — not a common combination in Scotland.

Below: Strathtay was the last big user of standard SBG Leopards with Alexander Y-type bodies. This pair are seen in Arbroath in 2001, by which time they had been relegated to school services.

2005 could still be seen on former SBG Leyland Tigers and MCW Metrobuses with Alexander bodies, the latter complete with SBG's trademark triangular destination display. It was also carried by some of the unusual ex-NBC long-wheelbase Leyland Olympian coaches, built for London commuter services and ending their days on limited-stop services between Cumbernauld and Glasgow.

First Glasgow also has an isolated pocket of operation in Ayrshire, a legacy of bus battles with Stagecoach in the 1990s. It uses a fleet of low-floor Dennis Darts with unusual UVG bodies.

North of Edinburgh, Fife Scottish Omnibuses is one company whose territory has changed little since the formation of the Alexander (Fife) company over 40 years ago. The company has been owned by Stagecoach since 1991 and today runs a modern fleet of standard Stagecoach vehicles, interspersed with a few survivors from SBG days in the shape of Volvo Citybuses. In round numbers Fife Scottish operates 300 buses, which is pretty much the same as when Stagecoach bought the business 15 years ago, if a marked reduction on the 500-plus vehicles which the company had in its heyday.

Aside from Arriva only two English-based operators have bus businesses in Scotland, and coincidentally both are based in Dundee. Travel Dundee is the former Tayside Regional Council bus operation, which was privatised in 1991 and bought by National Express in 1997. And Strathtay Scottish

has since 1991 been owned by Yorkshire Traction, being the only company in the SBG privatisation process to be sold to an English buyer.

Travel Dundee made the news at the end of 2004 when it became the first major British urban operator to have converted its route network to 100% low-floor operation. The vehicles that allowed this to happen were the fleet's first batch of new double-deckers since 1989 — a batch of Volvo B7TLs with Wrightbus bodies identical to those being delivered to parent company Travel West Midlands.

Appropriately Travel Dundee's predecessor, Tayside Regional Transport, had been the first Scottish operator of a low-floor bus when it took delivery of an East Lancs-bodied Scania N113 in 1993. In the current fleet there are a range of low-floor types, including the relatively rare Volvo B10L.

Strathtay Scottish is one former SBG subsidiary which is still clearly identifiable. Most of the others, even if still recognisably serving the same territory, have become subsumed in the corporate colours of Stagecoach, First and Arriva. The only other exception is Highland, which as part of the Rapson Group has retained a distinctive identity, albeit in a blue livery which breaks with the use of various shades of red used by the company until quite recently.

The Strathtay fleet is based in Dundee and serves the area to the north of the city. It originally also served Perth but withdrew its local services there after a battle with Stagecoach, which has its headquarters in the city.

Strathtay runs 160 buses, which range from assorted minibuses and Leyland Tigers (some rebodied by East Lancs) through to Dennis Darts, Volvo Olympians and low-floor Volvo B7TLs. The newest double-deckers all have East Lancs bodies.

Aberdeen is the headquarters of First, and thereby hangs one of the most remarkable tales of modern transport history — how a management buy-out at Grampian Regional Transport grew to be a major international bus and train operator.

First Aberdeen is the direct descendant of Grampian Regional Transport and is the main operator of city services, running a network which in places can be traced back to the bus and tram services of Aberdeen Corporation Transport.

Most of First Aberdeen's buses are Volvo B10BLEs, but there are also a few B7LA artics and B7TL double-deckers. The B10BLEs include some

with unusual, for First, Alexander ALX300 bodies. These started life in Glasgow. The oldest buses are former GRT Olympians with Alexander R-type bodies.

Stagecoach Bluebird is the successor to Northern Scottish and serves Aberdeen's hinterland and the area stretching westwards to Inverness and thence north to Tain. Inter-urban services are operated by Volvo coaches, including a fleet of Plaxton-bodied B7Rs — the group's first — delivered in 2005. Among the standard Stagecoach Darts and MANs are Volvo Olympians with Northern Counties bodies, some bought new and some transferred from the company's London fleets.

The Inverness operations marked expansion by Stagecoach following a bus war at the start of the 1990s. The loser was Highland Scottish, which for many years was the sole provider of town services in Inverness but is now primarily a rural operator. Highland's post-privatisation history is a tortuous one, but suffice it to say that what was the bulk of

Below: There are relatively few double-deckers with First Aberdeen. The oldest are 10 Alexander-bodied Olympians which were new to Grampian in 1988.

Right: In northeast Scotland Stagecoach initially made use of the Bluebird motif, which had been synonymous with Alexander's coach operations since the 1930s. This Olympian with Alexander body was new to Northern Scottish in 1987.

Left: The current generation of Stagecoach Bluebird buses includes TransBus Pointer Darts, as seen here in Inverness in 2004.

Right: An ex-Nottingham City Transport Mercedes-Benz 811D with Plaxton Beaver body typifies the small buses which make up much of the Highland fleet. It is seen loading in Inverness bus station in 2004.

the Highland business, serving an area from Fort William in the south to Wick and Thurso in the north, is now run by the Rapson group.

It's a vast area, with few towns of any size, and the fleet is made up largely of second-hand vehicles which include ex-West Midlands Lynxes and ex-Lothian Olympians, as well as older types such as Bristol VRTs. More modern acquisitions include Alexander-bodied Dennis Dart SLFs and Optare Excels, and there are vehicles bought new too, including 70-seat Plaxton-bodied Javelins and a Wrightbus-bodied VDL SB200, which is a rare type in Scotland. Long-distance services are operated by Volvo B10M coaches.

In many ways Scotland's buses look more standardised in the commercialised industry created by the legislation of two decades ago than they did before. You can see Stagecoach corporate colours from Dumfries in the south to Tain in the north. First's influence extends from the Scottish Borders to Aberdeen — and it runs the trains too.

What of the Conservative aim of a multiplicity of small operators? Well, these exist too. Greenock is served exclusively by small companies. There are independents in Paisley. In the Glasgow area, McKindless and Henderson are two operators who have established bus operations in the last two decades. And, of course, even Stagecoach started off as a small player in the bus business. Who would have thought 20 years ago that a company running Magic Bus Routemasters in competition with the mighty Strathclyde PTE bus operation on a Glasgow local service would grow to become a major international transport business?

Right: An unusual type in Scotland is the VDL SB200 with Wrightbus Commander body. Rapsons took one in 2004 for the service between Inverness and Fort George via the airport.

Left: Small operators come and go. White Star, operating in the south of Scotland, was taken over by Stagecoach in 2003. A Stagecoach fleet number is just visible on this Plaxton-bodied Dennis Dart in Moffat.

Ramblings on Ribble in the 'Seventies

Working at Ribble during the early 1970s gave ALLAN EDMONDSON a view not only of a company in transition but also of a change in the shape of the industry.

When even the privatisation of NBC seems an event in the distant past, memories of the constituent companies that made up that august body seem even further away, kept alive only by preserved vehicles in the liveries of a bygone age. I don't think of myself as being old, but not only do I remember the pre-NBC era; I actually worked in it, and some would say it was at an exciting time, as it all was soon to change forever.

I joined Ribble Motor Services in August 1970, having been successful in gaining a place in its well-respected Traffic Apprentice scheme. This was a revelation — a five-year course in which, I was told, it was essential for me to know how to do every job in the company, from being a conductor to running a depot. I would do it all.

At this time Ribble was still just about the biggest bus company in Britain, with an operating territory that reached from the Scottish border in the north down to Merseyside in the south. It provided rural services along country lanes and urban services in some of the most densely-populated regions at the time, coupled with a network of express services that were the envy of the industry and incorporated innovation with efficiency.

By the time I became ensconced, the big moment had already quietly arrived. Following the Transport Act 1968, Ribble, previously a BET subsidiary, had, in January 1969, become part of the National Bus Company, but on the surface there was little change. United's operations in Carlisle had been transferred to Ribble in an early

Left: Atlantean coaches were used on a number of inter-urban express services. There were 20, delivered in 1962 with 59-seat Weymann bodies.
Allan Edmondson

Right: The older double-deckers in the Ribble fleet were all Leyland Titans. New in 1955, this PD2 had a Metro-Cammell Orion body and was one of the last survivors of 45 delivered that year. It was withdrawn from service in 1972.
Allan Edmondson

Left: Unusual coaches in the Ribble fleet were two Leyland Leopards acquired in 1963 from Michelin Tyres — with only the Stoke-on-Trent registration numbers to give the game away, at a time when new Ribble coaches were registered in Preston. They had handsome Plaxton Panorama bodies and were less than 12 months old when purchased by Ribble.
Allan Edmondson

rationalisation move, but to the untrained eye much of the business remained the same.

Even vehicle repaints at that time didn't give any clues as to what would happen in the future. Being based at the head office at Frenchwood, Preston, I had a perfect view to see what was coming and going out of the central works and the paintshops. Newly outshopped vehicles sported the newer fleetname, with lower-case lettering, but still retained their traditional dark-red livery.

Likewise, vehicle deliveries until now had remained on traditional lines, although there had already been a 'toe in the water' exercise in BET days with the acquisition in 1968 of Bristol RELL/ECWs; previously such vehicles had, of course, been available only to Tilling companies.

But, looking back, it was clear things were changing. Bristol and ECW had been commissioned to produce an updated double-deck coach for use on Standerwick's Lancashire–London services, to replace the 'Gay Hostess' Atlanteans. Following the launch of the prototype Bristol VRL coach at the Commercial Motor Show in 1968, production versions appeared in 1971.

On the bus front, the further march of the Bristol/ECW combination had manifested itself with the introduction of VRTs. I well recall the excitement we enthusiasts felt as we saw something never seen before! But still they were in traditional Ribble livery, and very smart they looked too.

But by now something was stirring in the paintshops, and it became an essential requirement

Right: In the year before the author joined Ribble the company had taken over the Carlisle operations of United. This ex-United Bristol MW5G is seen in its previous owner's colours — Tilling red — but with Ribble fleetname and number in Carlisle in August 1969. The bus was new in 1962 and was one of 21 vehicles acquired from United. *R. L. Wilson*

Left: The modern double-deckers in the Ribble fleet were Leyland Atlanteans. Still in Ribble dark red in 1974, this Northern Counties-bodied bus was one of 15 low-height PDR1/2 models delivered in 1967. *Stewart J. Brown*

Below left: With the Isle of Skye behind it a Ribble Leopard stands on the slipway at Kyleakin in 1972. It has a luxurious 36-seat Plaxton Panorama Elite body and was one of 25 delivered in the year the author started working for Ribble. *Stewart J. Brown*

each lunchtime for us to have a look at what was emerging. As part of the ongoing NBC-ising of the company a complex agreement had been reached with Crosville to exchange routes in the Merseyside area. A definite sign that Ribble had newly adopted brothers was the invasion of the paintshop by Bristols and AECs which belonged to Crosville and SELNEC Cheshire (formally North Western), resulting in some unusual combinations of vehicle type and livery.

At around this time the Chairman of NBC, Freddie Wood, issued an edict that outlined the organisation's requirements in terms of corporate image. (Bear in mind that I didn't even know what the term meant!) We learned as staff that vehicles were to be painted in a peculiar shade of red, well-known now, of course, as poppy red. Coaches would be in all-over white but with the constituent company's name in tiny letters above the front wheel-arch. There was a twist to this tale when, as an experiment, one of the Bristol VRL coaches was painted in a very attractive blue and white. However, after only a few weeks in service it was repainted in all over white, which in this writer's view made a very attractive vehicle appear frumpy and, quite honestly, ruined its lines.

Above: Although Bristol VRLs were being delivered, an earlier generation of double-deck motorway coaches was still in evidence at the start of the 1970s. This Standerwick Atlantean in London's Victoria Coach Station was new in 1961 and had a 50-seat Weymann body. *Stewart J. Brown*

Below: Ribble's fleet in the early 1970s included a large number of Leyland Titan PD3s with distinctive full-fronted forward-entrance bodies by Burlingham or, as on this bus in Liverpool, Metro-Cammell. *Stewart J. Brown*

Left: Strange vehicles to appear in Ribble's paintshops were former North Western buses which had been acquired by Crosville at the start of 1972 and which were sent to Preston to be repainted green. This is a 1963 AEC Renown with 74-seat Park Royal body.
Allan Edmondson

Right: NBC corporate poppy red spread across the fleet from 1972, as seen on this 1962 Atlantean in Blackburn bus station in 1980. It had a lowbridge Metro-Cammell body. There were 14 buses in this batch, and they were Ribble's last lowbridge buses. They were withdrawn in 1981/2.
Stewart J. Brown

Left: Ribble's second batch of Bristol RELLs was delivered in 1969 and comprised 30 buses, all with dual-door ECW bodywork. When new they were in Ribble dark red, but by 1974 they had been repainted in poppy red. One is seen in Lord Street, Southport.
Stewart J. Brown

Right: By no stretch of the imagination was this Weymann-bodied Leyland Leopard a luxury coach, and it's tempting to think that in painting it in National white someone in the Ribble hierarchy was protesting about the new corporate livery. Most NBC coaches with this style of body were painted in local-coach livery with, in Ribble's case, the lower half of the body in poppy red. *Allan Edmondson*

Left: Ribble's first Leyland Nationals were delivered in 1972 in the company's established dark red but were repainted poppy red before entering service. The second, of a batch of 15, is seen at Frenchwood immediately after delivery in November 1972. *Allan Edmondson*

Right: The first new Ribble coaches in National white were 10 Bristol RELH6Ls with 49-seat ECW bodies, delivered in the autumn of 1972. *Allan Edmondson*

Further change was in the air as the Leyland National commenced production, and Ribble was one of the first companies to receive the type. Amidst much anticipation, the first deliveries duly rolled in, gloriously finished in Ribble dark red! However, they quickly disappeared into the paintshop and reappeared soon after, resplendent in corporate poppy red and with the fleetname in the new NBC standard style.

New coach deliveries reflected the new NBC structure, as Bristol RELH/ECW coaches were delivered in the new all-over white. Limited to working shorter-haul routes, they complemented the Leopards that made up the core of the coach fleet.

To many enthusiasts — me included — the colourful collection of coaches at seaside locations at the height of the summer season was an awe-inspiring sight. There was a myriad of liveries and vehicle types; but fast-forward a couple of years, and most of them had been changed to the bland uniformity of NBC white.

The image changes had by now permeated throughout the Ribble organisation. To the outsider the biggest change was the addition of the 'double N' logo and NBC corporate lettering on timetables and literature.

However, the story is not just about vehicles; it is also about the monolithic and almost surreal size of the business and how it operated in the early

1970s. This was a monster company, with a huge head office at Frenchwood and a fully integrated in-house business operation. Everything, from the design of timetables to the planning of routes and schedules, was undertaken in this huge building and done with military precision. Of course, many of the senior managers had come to Ribble from serving in the war, so it was no surprise really to see that, but nonetheless it is strange in retrospect, particularly since Ribble is now but a shadow of its former self.

I was seconded to the Express Service department for longer than the usual trainee's allocated time, as I enjoyed myself there and it coincided with a busy summer season in 1972.

Whilst it seems antiquated now, the system known as 'ABC' or Advanced Booking Control was really quite sophisticated. Booking agents issuing tickets for express services would send pink copies of the tickets in an envelope to Ribble's head office, where they would be charted — a process simply noting the numbers of passengers on each individual journey chart — and an assessment made as to the number of vehicles required for a particular service and any duplicate vehicles ordered. Once the basic framework of duplication had been created, it was then left to the local managers to fill in the gaps as necessary. On tours and excursions, it was a marvel to see how the itineraries were planned, right down to the last detail, and published on a running-sheet that would be followed by the driver from the allocated depot.

As part of the newly formed NBC Ribble played a huge role in being one of the first bus companies to make full use of the new computer technology. As I write this on a laptop it seems almost incredible to think that the computer installed at Frenchwood three decades ago filled a room larger in floor area than the entire ground floor of my house. Staff had to wear hairnets and shoe covers to prevent dust from affecting the magnetic disks — all this just (at its first level of operation) to do the wages! Later it would be expanded to undertake joint-service data-processing and the accounts function and also to do similar work for Crosville and others.

By the summer of 1974 things were really beginning to change. The coaching activities of Ribble, North Western and Standerwick became National Travel (West), with operational offices in Manchester and Blackpool. Similar reorganisations occurred in other operational territories, and it was the start of the demise of many locally recognised famous coaching names such as Sheffield United Tours and Black & White of Cheltenham. It would

be the pivotal move that created the National Express empire we know today.

Me? Well, the formation of NBC created with it a new training scheme designed for graduates and intended to 'fast-track' bright, youthful managers into the newly nationalised industry. This rendered obsolescent the in-house schemes of companies like Ribble, and in order to pursue my own interests in coaching I moved firstly to National Travel but then, in 1978, to the independent sector.

I feel very privileged to have worked for Ribble. It was an organisation of immense pride and character, and many of the things I learned at Ribble still have relevance today. It was an interesting time, although memories are tinged with sadness that this once-great company — it ran well over 1,000 vehicles when I joined it — was split up and emasculated by the development of NBC.

Ironically, I was to have further experience of the NBC right at its end, as part of the management buy-out team of Wessex National, in Bristol — but that's a whole different story!

Below: Coach operations featured prominently in the author's time at Ribble. New coaches delivered during his time with the company included 19 Leyland Leopards with 49 seat Duple Dominant bodies, in 1973. New in overall white, they later received NBC's so called 'venetian blind' livery, with a red and blue slatted pattern. One waits for passengers outside Preston station in 1983.
Stewart J. Brown

Gone but Not Forgotten

GEOFF MILLS illustrates a selection of well-known operators which have vanished, covering the period from the 1960s to the 1990s.

Left: In 1963 Moore's of Kelvedon sold out to Eastern National. This scene, in Duke Street, Chelmsford, was recorded just days before the company changed hands and features a 1949 Guy Arab III which had recently — in 1960 — been fitted with a new Massey body. Massey bodywork, built in Wigan, was popular with a number of small operators around this time.

Right: Bamber Bridge Motor Services operated between that town and Preston until selling out to Ribble in 1967. Its small fleet included this former demonstration Albion Lowlander with Alexander body, which had been exhibited at the 1961 Scottish Motor Show in the livery of Glasgow Corporation Transport. It was one of three Bamber Bridge vehicles to be taken over by Ribble, for which it operated until 1975.

Right: Samuel Ledgard of Leeds sold out to West Yorkshire in October 1967, at which time its fleet included this shining Weymann-bodied AEC Regent V. The bus had been new to South Wales Transport.

Left: This AEC Regent III with unusual forward-entrance lowbridge Roe bodywork was operated by Liss & District and is seen in Bordon in 1961. Liss & District was associated with the Creamline group, which ceased operating in 1967.

Right: Birch Bros was a company with a long history. It ran both bus and coach services, and its bus operations ceased in 1969, being taken over by United Counties. This 1946 Leyland Titan PD1 with 1956 Metro-Cammell Orion body, seen at Birch's Harlow depot in 1961, was one of seven similarly rebodied PD1s which were the last double-deckers run by Birch. Double-deck operation ceased in 1967.

Right: King Alfred of Winchester disappeared over 30 years ago but is fondly remembered by enthusiasts of a certain age. In the early 1950s it was buying new Leyland Titans; photographed in Winchester in 1967, this all-Leyland PD2 was new in 1950 and would give King Alfred 20 years of service. Hants & Dorset bought King Alfred in 1973.

Left: In 1973 Derby Corporation took over the business of Blue Bus of Willington — a rare acquisition (at that time) of a private business by a local authority. Blue Bus operated 23 vehicles, including 11 double-deckers, nine of which were Daimlers. The oldest was this 1953 CD650 with lowbridge Willowbrook body, seen in Derby in 1973 with a Corporation CVG6 in the background.

Right: There is a Green Bus company operating in Staffordshire and the West Midlands in 2005, but there was an earlier company of that name, which was taken over by Midland Red in 1973. This Foden PVD6 with 53 seat Samlesbury body had been bought new in 1949 and is seen here in 1963 with exhaust emissions that presumably reflect a cold start on a winter's day rather than the maintenance standards of its owner.

Left: Blue Ensign was one of a number of Doncaster-area independents which sold out to South Yorkshire PTE in the 1970s. In 1960 its fleet included an ex-Glasgow Corporation AEC Regent with Weymann body. New in 1938, it had been bought by Blue Ensign in 1951 and would survive until 1963.

Right: Another Doncaster operator acquired by South Yorkshire PTE in the 1970s was Premier of Stainforth. Premier regularly bought new double-deckers and in 1959 took this Guy Arab with 65-seat Roe body. At that time the forward-entrance layout was unusual for a small operator. Premier's buses were painted in an attractive two-tone-blue and cream.

Left: Burwell & District operated both new and second-hand Daimler Fleetlines. The latter included six ex-Nottingham buses, one of which was this 1963 example with 77-seat Northern Counties body, photographed in 1976. Burwell & District was bought by Eastern Counties in 1979.

Right: Lockey's of West Auckland was one of a number of small operators in County Durham and had a distinctive black livery. This ex London RTL was an impressive 23 years old when photographed in Bishop Auckland in June 1972, still looking very smart. Lockey's was taken over by OK Motor Services in 1983 and operated as a subsidiary until 1985.

Left: Rees & Williams of Tycroes operated this smart Massey-bodied Guy Arab II. The chassis dated from 1946; the body from 1955. It is seen in Swansea in 1965. D Coaches of Morriston bought the Rees & Williams business in 1988.

Right: This Guy Arab IV with Strachans body was one of the exhibits at the 1962 Commercial Motor Show. Its owner was Graham's Bus Service of Paisley, a long-standing Guy user, although this was to be the company's last new Guy and, indeed, the last for a Scottish operator. Strachans had only just re-entered the double-deck market. This is a 1972 view. Graham's closed in 1990, unable to survive in the post-1986 deregulated environment.

Above: York Pullman evoked a certain quality, both in its choice of name and in the presentation of its vehicles. It was often associated with AECs, and this Roe-bodied Regent III was new in 1954. It is seen in York in 1963. York Pullman changed hands in 1985, becoming Reynard Pullman.

Below: South Notts generally bought new buses, but there were second-hand vehicles in the fleet too, such as this ex-Ribble Leyland Titan, which it operated between 1960 and 1964. The chassis, a TD5, dated from 1939, while the Alexander body had been fitted in 1949. The South Notts business, based in Gotham, was purchased by Nottingham City Transport in 1991.

Left: Norfolk's of Nayland was a company with a long history, finally being taken over in 1991 by Hedingham & District. This vehicle, an ex-SELNEC PTE Daimler Fleetline with Park Royal body, was sold a few months before Hedingham bought the business. The deep windscreens which characterised these Manchester Corporation-designed bodies have been replaced by less expensive — and more readily available — BET screens, radically altering the appearance of the vehicle. It has also acquired an early-1960s Daimler badge.

Left: The A1 Service co-operative was taken over by Stagecoach in 1995, but this view is of an earlier era. In the late 1950s and early 1960s A1's members bought large numbers of redundant London Transport RTs and RTLs, and this RTL was extensively rebuilt, with a forward entrance and staircase. It is seen in the A1 bus station in Ardrossan in 1972.

Left: OK Motor Services was an interesting operation, with a varied fleet over the years. This is a 1971 view, showing an ex-Brighton Hove & District Bristol KSW6G in Bishop Auckland market place. OK was taken over by the Go Ahead-Group in 1995.

Right: The number of independent operators serving Paisley declined gradually from the 1960s, and after the closure of Graham's in 1990 just one of the old names was left — although plenty of new ones had arrived. The last survivor of the old order was McGill's of Barrhead, with a smart fleet of buses, most of which were bought new. For many years the company's services were operated by double-deckers, and these included this ex demonstration Daimler CVG6-30 with 74-seat Willowbrook body. It was the only 30ft Daimler to have a Birmingham-style 'new look' front. McGill's sold out to Cowie's Clydeside business in 1997.

Left: Grey-Green was originally a coach operator but in the 1980s became increasingly involved in London bus operation. Most of its buses were bought new, but for some London contracts it purchased used vehicles. These included MCW Metrobuses, such as this ex-Newport Transport example seen in Romford in 1995. Grey-Green was latterly owned by Cowie, which metamorphosed into Arriva. It became part of Arriva London in 1998.

Right: Harris of Grays was a respected coach operator which, like Grey-Green, also diversified into buses in the 1980s. Its early operations were in Essex, and by 1991 its fleet included this ex-Northampton Bristol VRT with Alexander body — an unusual combination — seen at the Lakeside shopping centre. Harris expanded its bus operations rapidly in the mid-1990s — too rapidly, as it turned out; the bus business closed in 2000.

The Long Goodbye

All photographs by the author

PETER ROWLANDS feels his photography has been charting the demise of Routemasters for most of his life. Reluctantly he braces himself for vanishing-point.

It's a bright, blustery morning in January 2005. I'm standing on Putney Bridge Approach, watching a number 14 bus rounding the bend from Fulham High Street and passing the corner of New King's Road. And I'm wondering exactly what I'm looking at.

Well, it's a Routemaster bus — that's for sure. It's RML2590, to be precise. But it's more than that. It's a symbol. A statement. An anomaly. An icon. I can't somehow believe this is the last January I'll ever see Routemasters on their original routes in London streets.

It seems to be true, though. I was in Oxford Street last week, and they were gone. I can hardly convey the shock of emerging from the Underground into a Routemasterless world. I found it was possible to stand for minutes at a time without seeing a single example. It was as if the street had been drained of colour and character.

Returning home, I had to pull out some pictures I took there two summers ago, to convince myself I hadn't hallucinated the whole thing. Yes, there was the evidence: dozens and dozens of Routemasters — a tide of rounded red — stretching away to vanishing-point. They looked so *permanent*, so unassailable. And this is 2003 we're talking about here; keep that in mind. How could they virtually all disappear in the year and a half since then?

Maybe you consider Routemasters simply old, tired, outdated, noisy, draughty, inconvenient to board and cramped and heavy to drive? Potentially dangerous, even? I've heard all that, and I can see the arguments. It's a matter of perennial bafflement to me that in this cautious, safety-obsessed, politically correct age we still have passenger vehicles in service with no external doors. I suspect social historians will look back on this with disbelief.

But that's not the point really, is it? For those of us who are interested and keen, Routemasters have been the backdrop of our lives. If you're under 50 years old there have been Routemasters on London streets for your entire life. We can't have aged that much, can we, if the kind of bus our parents went to school on is still there in front of

Left: Oxford Street in May 2003 — full of now-vanished Routemasters, including the very last, RML2760, seen here at Marble Arch on its way to Paddington.

Left: This shot of a Leyland Titan PD2 of Halton Transport is one of the author's first-ever bus pictures. It was taken in Widnes in May 1977.

Below left: Blackpool's Metro-Cammell-bodied Leyland PD3s were among the last survivors of their type. This one is seen in Fleetwood in July 1977, with tram tracks in the foreground. It would last several years more.

Below: Hartlepool was still running a few Roe bodied Leyland PD2s until the late 1970s. This one is seen in July 1978.

us? Nor will we ever grow old — not as long as they are still there to reassure us.

Jump back 35 years, and I was of a rather different mind. For a start, it hadn't yet dawned on me that photographing buses was an acceptable pursuit. I was interested, yes, but merely as a bystander.

I grew up in Newcastle, where they stopped buying front-engined buses at the end of the 1950s. In my innocence I thought other bus operators must have followed suit. Then in 1970 I started travelling to other parts of the country, and, wonder of wonders, I found other towns and cities full of nearly new front-engined buses. It turned out they had been built right up until 1968, when new legislation on driver-only operation effectively

brought their production to an end. Places like Northampton and Blackpool had no rear-engined double-deckers at all. I was amazed.

Birmingham was full of buses that I thought had died out years before — those crazy, narrow, wobbly Daimlers and Guys. Newcastle had run a few early examples of these, but they were long gone. Greater Manchester still had an enormous array of front-engined makes and types. So did Glasgow; I discovered models like Albion Lowlanders whose very existence had hitherto passed me by.

I'd say it was 1977 when I finally felt that photographing buses for pleasure was my destiny, and by then even those more recent front-engined double-deckers were approaching the end of their

Left: Immaculately turned-out Bristol Lodekkas were a familiar sight on long routes like the Eastern National 251 between Southend and Wood Green.

Below left: Southampton's East Lancs-bodied AEC Regent Vs were late survivors of the type. These are seen in June 1979.

Below: Northern General, the only operator outside London to buy new Routemasters, still had them in service in October 1977, when this one was photographed in Newcastle in corporate NBC livery.

Right: Lancashire United Transport was a late and enthusiastic user of Guy Arabs. This Northern Counties-bodied example is seen outside its garage in Atherton in 1977.

lives. I felt a rising sense of panic: could I catch them before they all disappeared?

I wish I could say yes, but it would be a lie. I couldn't always dictate the times when I travelled or where my journeys would take me, and too often it wasn't where the best buses ran. Which is why I missed Exeter's last AECs, missed Reading's too; even missed Luton's Dennis Lolines, though they weren't that far from London (my adopted home). But steadily I filled in some of the other gaps — Daimler CVGs, Leyland Titans, AEC Regents and Renowns, Dennis Lolines, Bristol Lodekkas.

It's strange now to realise what a parsimonious attitude I had to photography in those days. One summer Saturday in 1980, on a visit to Cambridge, I set off to photograph buses in Norwich. It was a fairly long drive, and not one I was likely to make

again in the near future; yet according to my picture collection, despite spending a good half-day in the city, I took fewer than 20 photographs all told. Twenty! And that's including the duds. All that time and effort for so little result. Why?

What did strike me about Norwich was the presence of Bristol Lodekka variants I'd never seen before, including rare FL models. That's the version built with a long wheelbase but with the entrance at the back. They were mixed in a seemingly random way with more common FS (short) versions and FLF models (long, with forward entrance). You'd think I'd have gone into photographic overdrive. What can I tell you?

It was all over in about five years. One by one the operators of those surviving front-engined double-deckers withdrew them as one-person operation

became the norm. By the early 1980s only a few operators, such as Blackpool and Greater Manchester, still had any, and even these wouldn't last much longer. I felt a sense of loss, though not of surprise. In many ways it still seemed a miracle that such vehicles had survived so long. It was a goodbye I was expecting.

London Transport, of course, was the exception to all this; it still had its entire fleet of over 2,000 Routemasters in service. Until 1979 it was even operating some of the previous generation — RTs, dating from the early 1950s. That meant I was just in time to take a few pictures of these — although I didn't get enough, of course. The urgency somehow didn't impress itself on me until it was almost too late. I made half-hearted pilgrimages to Crystal Palace, Northolt and Rainham, and took inconclusive pictures of those that remained. And then they were gone. I turned up to the last RT journey in Barking in 1979 and proffered my ritual

farewell, but it was too little too late. And besides, the capital was still full of Routemasters. Or would they now go too?

They should have, and in the early 1980s a half-hearted Routemaster-withdrawal programme started. The first to disappear were some of the shorter-wheelbase RMs, by and large the older models, with their lower seating capacity. And I have to say that I took this in my stride. I never really believed they could last forever, even if I secretly wished they would.

However, LT also had to contend with its little-loved Fleetline rear-engined double-deckers from the 1970s, which it considered costly and unreliable. And instead of pursuing a comprehensive Routemaster replacement programme it focused on rooting out those. In came the Metrobus and the Titan, and, as if unnoticed, Routemasters soldiered on.

Meanwhile many of London's discarded Routemasters suddenly started to find a second life in other UK towns and cities. Bus deregulation was by now in full swing, and more and more operators decided that second-hand Routemasters could be their secret weapon in the battle for customers. Eventually a dozen major operators had them in service, from Perth and Glasgow down to Southampton.

Below left: An FLF Lodekka near the end of its life with Eastern Counties in Norwich in April 1980.

Below: Greater Manchester PTE inherited numerous half-cab double-deckers from constituent operators and was still running some of them in the 1980s. This is an East Lancs-bodied Leyland PD3, new to Stockport Corporation, at Piccadilly station.

Above: Looking confusingly as if on service in London, RM378 is seen here at Manchester's Piccadilly in October 1988 during its relatively short stay in the city.

Below: Strathtay managed to produce a remarkably convincing facsimile of a traditional municipal livery For its Perth-based Routemaster fleet. This example is seen in November 1989.

Right: Southend Transport's Routemaster fleet ran for several years around the end of the 1980s. This one is seen in the operator's crisp blue livery in December 1988.

Left: Before the emergence of Stagecoach's ubiquitous corporate livery Routemasters on its Bedford services wore this green livery with '*Routemaster*' fleetnames, as here in May 1988.

Right: 'Mitcham — Cricketers' was the familiar destination of the 88, seen here in October 1987.

Above: The 29 would soon lose its Routemasters when this picture was taken at Parliament Square in July 1987.

Below: The 25 used to make the trek from Victoria through to Becontree Heath. This early Routemaster shows the battered domes that were familiar before glass-fibre versions alleviated the problem.

Above: Prior to massive redevelopment at Hammersmith in the early 1990s the 11 terminated here, but the route was later cut back to Fulham Broadway. The 11 was one of the first routes to go in the final cull. This example, with non-standard Leyland badge, is seen in May 1989.

This was very strange. Provincial half-cab buses had hitherto come in all shapes, sizes and makes; now they were all Routemasters. The general public even came to refer to them by that name.

I decided to make it my business to photograph and video them in their new homes and managed to accumulate a pretty reasonable selection of still and moving pictures. I have to say though that I couldn't take these buses all that seriously. Some — the maroon examples in Perth, for instance, or the dark-blues in Hull — made a good stab at evoking the flavour of an earlier era, while the crisp blues in Southend showed how effective they could look in more modern turnout. But you knew it was all impermanent and somehow fake. And, sure enough, by the start of the 'Nineties they were being withdrawn. Goodbye again, I thought, but with no great surprise.

By rights the rest of London's own Routemasters should have been confronting large-scale withdrawal as well. By the late 1980s all Routemasters were between 20 and 30 years old — at least twice the normal projected age of a typical bus — and the withdrawal programme stuttered back into action (it had never entirely stopped). Famous routes that had survived the previous cull now came under new threat: the 2B and 3 down to Norwood and Crystal Palace; the 88 to Mitcham; the 29 from Victoria to Enfield; the 149 from Waterloo to Ponders End, run latterly by refurbished Country RCLs, with their peculiar rear ends now bereft of the platform doors with which had been fitted when they operated as coaches.

This time I was ready. I was waiting. I wasn't going to miss out on my photographic farewells again. At midnight on the last day of the 29 I was there in Enfield Town with my video camera on a tripod. I went to Mitcham to see the Cricketers pub made famous by the destination indicator. I went out to Romford to see where the 25 ended up, and traced the 36B to Lewisham.

I was also galvanised by decisions to curtail certain Routemaster routes. Months before the 22 route was cut in half I was in Hackney, making sure could prove that Routemasters once ran right through from Putney — a prodigious journey, and one to rival the more recently lamented 73. I went up to Finchley while the 13 still did. I went down to Barnes Bridge when route 9 still ran alongside the Thames to Mortlake. I discovered the perennial pointlessness of ferreting out back-street termini.

By now the half-cab era had already run way beyond its time, and should have ended. But, as we know, that's not what happened. As the 1990s

Above: One of Stagecoach's immaculate Routemasters crossing Ludgate Circus in July 1995 on the famous route 8 to Bow.

unfolded a new status quo had settled on London's bus scene. London Transport's bus operations had been 'divisionalised' and then sold off, and the various buyers had sold out or been acquired by rivals. Yet route-tendering continued to specify Routemasters, so the leading operators all kept their contingents of them. Sometimes newcomers to the scene had to obtain them — notably Kentish Bus and what became Sovereign. London Transport (later TfL) kept its own float.

For much of the 1990s and well into the 2000s there were roundly 20 Routemaster routes, requiring upwards of 700 buses in all (including short-wheelbase RMs, which against expectation survived almost to the last). It was an amusing diversion to run mentally through the routes — every one from 6 to 15, then 19, 22, 23, 36, 38 and so on. Walking along Oxford Street, I used to tick off the routes mentally as I saw them and photographed them, reassuring myself they were still there. And photograph them I did — just to make sure…

By the early 2000s it seemed this state of affairs had existed forever. Then along came Mayor

Ken Livingstone — initially the Routemaster's staunchest ally, then suddenly its scourge. By 2004 it was plain he wanted them gone, and they would go.

And suddenly I'm transported back 20 years or more. The same agony of withdrawal is happening all over again. Another route disappears; last journeys are celebrated; enthusiasts flock to the wake. The 11, the 8, the 15 — famous journeys that cross the heart of London. There's a striking difference from previous withdrawals of this kind: the last RTs were relegated to the outer suburbs; Routemasters, by contrast, have been running right to the end on London's most high-profile and intensive routes.

Down go the 137, the 73, the 9, the 12 — routes that seem to embody the Routemaster spirit. As I write this there are seven Routemaster routes left — the 13, the 14, 19, the 22, the 36, the 38 and the 159. Two of these, the 19 and the 36, will be gone by spring 2005. By the time you read this there may be none left at all.

There's a shocking abruptness to their departure. Usually vehicle types are withdrawn over a long period — especially when, as here, there are more than 500 examples in service. It seemed only reasonable to suppose that this kind of phased withdrawal would be the pattern with the surviving Routemasters. Despite their extraordinary age they

Right: Sympathetic livery treatment for this former Green Line RMC coach, which for some years operated on Stagecoach's route 15. This view in Oxford Street was recorded in June 1996.

Below: London General's RML2680 is seen here in the City on the 11 in July 1999. It transferred to the 14/22 group when the 11 was converted in 2003.

have been so much re-engined and refurbished that those still running could undoubtedly run on for many years to come.

Instead, they are being withdrawn with relentless single-mindedness. Within the space of less than two years the whole lot will be gone. Seeing them go is like seeing a disconsolate child throwing out a plaything it has become bored with. Buses with a future as well as a past are being almost literally thrown away.

Remarkably, if you go to Piccadilly today, in January 2005, you can still see most of the Routemaster routes in action; a hint of the old order flickers on. But not for long.

Above: An RML on the 73 at Angel in August 2004, shortly before conversion of the route to articulated operation.

Below: The 159 was one of the last five Routemaster routes, and buses on it ended up looking notably dowdy. In smarter times, RM2217 turns into Regent Street in August 1998.

Left: Still in service on the 159 in September 1999, although looking somewhat battered, was Arriva's RM6, now in preservation.

Below: The 36 was an unlikely survivor after the 36B was converted to OPO in 1992. This shot was taken on Vauxhall Bridge in June 1993.

At least we now know answers to some of those trivial questions — like which will be the last Routemaster routes, or which individual vehicles will survive the longest. As I write, we don't know which will be the very last original route, but word on the street says it is the 38. Personally I'd have voted for the two routes on the 14/22 corridor, most of whose Routemasters were repainted around the turn of 2003/4 and still look superb. By the time you read this, presumably you will know.

Historians will no doubt debate why Routemasters lasted so long. Suffice it to say that enough advocates with the necessary political and operational clout were in the right place at the right time to make it possible. They made the choices, and we lived them.

So here I stand at Putney Bridge, caught up in this extraordinary phenomenon. It's absurd that Routemasters should still be here, yet totally unnerving to imagine them gone. I could put my hand out and stop this Routemaster, but I can't halt time. Somehow, the final withdrawal programme brings that helplessness home to me.

As JJD 590D pulls away from the bus stop and on to the bridge itself I raise my camera once again. Illogical, yes, but in a corner of my mind I was sure that Routemasters really would run forever. Now it's clear they won't — and however many pictures I have of them, it's not enough. This is one goodbye I won't be missing.

Saturday Night Weaver

Join the crush on the smoke-filled top deck as DAVID WAYMAN captures the essence of a late-night journey home in North East England at the close of the 1950s, when buses were busy, people smoked, and even drunks behaved themselves.

It would be a rush, but they didn't want to miss the twenty-five-past-ten bus. Not that it was Saturday night's final departure on service 40 from Newcastle, but they'd already had to abandon their original plan of catching the previous one at a quarter past ten. That bus would have enabled Mavis to make a quick onward connection in Sunderland with the last bus at 11 o'clock on local service 3 to her home on the outskirts of town. But by catching the 10.25pm from Newcastle instead, she would be able to do the next best thing: transfer to another bus on an inter-urban service, either the 49 leaving Sunderland (Waterloo Place) at 11.10 or the 57 at the same time from Sunderland (Park Lane bus station). Ever gallant, Boyfriend would of course accompany her to her door and never dream of doing otherwise.

They reached Newcastle's Worswick Street bus station and … oh good — the double-decker working the 10.25 service 40 journey was just about to leave. Oh, not good — it had a full, standing load, and a fair crowd was already queuing at the barrier for the next one at 10.35. Newcastle United had played at home that afternoon, and a multitude of supporters from outlying districts who had stayed in the 'toon' for an evening's refreshment were now making for home.

It was time for quick thinking. With the 10.25 gone, the 10.35 from Newcastle on service 40 would get them to Sunderland in time to catch a 49 at 11.20. *But they might not be able to get on the 10.35 at Newcastle.* Right, so what about the 10.27 from Newcastle to Sunderland on service 64, entailing a journey taking 11 minutes longer? They could use their return tickets, and at a pinch this bus could get them there in time to jump on that 11.20 number 49. Of course, like all the connections mooted, it depended on the fairly reasonable expectation of no delay to the bus from Newcastle

and a driver, eager to get home, practising to be a jet pilot from the last intermediate timing point (or — shh — even before it!). They decided to take the chance, for if the first part of the venture failed there would still be the last 49 at 11.30.

Almost ready to leave Newcastle, the bus on service 64 appeared to have a seat or two unoccupied. Climbing its stairs and then cutting their way through the acrid haze created by night-time smokers, they found a vacant double seat on the nearside, about the third along. This was a comfortable place to sit coughing. In the fleet of the Northern General Transport Co, known locally simply as Northern, the red and cream bus was No 1421, a heavyweight 56 seat Park Royal-bodied Guy Arab III, built six years previously, in 1952. As the 7.0-litre Gardner 5LW engine barked into life the conductor walked along the platform to remove the long-handled chock from under the nearside front wheel. Oh yes, Worswick Street bus station, with its steeply rising platforms running diagonally to the thoroughfare, had seen some spectacular run-backs into the wall behind and indeed would see still more on some occasions when the chock wasn't used.

With some effort the bus crawled forward in first gear, and when clear of the platform the driver made the usual snatch change into second for the few yards to the top of Worswick Street. Here 1421 did a left turn into Pilgrim Street, the A1 Edinburgh–London road, and headed south towards the spectacular Tyne Bridge, opened in 1928, with its roadway suspended from the giant steel parabolic arch structure. (Several of 1421's passengers were also parabolic, or something sounding vaguely similar …)

By crossing this bridge the bus left Newcastle and entered Gateshead. At that point too the River Tyne marked the boundary between Northumberland and

County Durham. One of Newcastle's claims to fame was a most attractive Corporation Transport & Electricity Undertaking fleet comprising 250 motor buses and 186 trolleybuses in an unusual livery of cadmium yellow and cream. Gateshead, however, could claim to be the home of many more buses. Not only were there the 70 of the Gateshead & District Omnibus Co, in a distinctive dark maroon with a little cream relief; there were Northern's 680, for that concern had its head office and a depot in the town, although much of the fleet was fostered to other depots, of course.

The bus stopped at the south end of the Tyne Bridge (0.7 mile, due there 10.31) to pick up a couple of revellers. Now, it was well known that open rear-entrance double-deckers had a stanchion in the middle of the edge of the platform. One of those boarding must have been seeing *two* stanchions, but as he tried to grab he missed them both and nearly redesigned the staircase with his head. What was that about delay? Well, fortuitously it turned out to be minimal (the poor bloke must

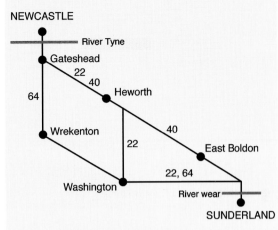

Bus services, Sunderland – Newcastle, 1957-58

have been anæsthetised, although he would never have managed to say that), and 1421 embarked on the long drag. This was the almost straight ascent from an altitude of 100ft at the bridge to 533ft in less than three miles, just before Wrekenton.

Only a few hundred yards to the west lay British Railways' large Gateshead Motive Power Depot (shed 52A), home to Class A4 Pacifics *Silver King*, *Golden Eagle* and other 'streaks'. And not far to the west of the shed lay the coal staiths on the

Below: Seen here in relatively new condition is 1418, a 1952 Park Royal-bodied Guy Arab III 5LW of the same batch of 20 as 'Saturday Night Weaver' No 1421. The well-proportioned lines of the London RT-derived body design are plain to see.
David Wayman collection

Above: The conductor removes the chock as a Sunderland District 1955 Metro Cammell Orion-bodied Leyland Titan PD2/12, one of five, prepares to leave Newcastle's Worswick Street bus station for West Hartlepool on service 40. *Roy Marshall*

Below: In the bright afternoon sunshine a Northern Arab 5LW, one of 20 delivered in 1952, heads onto the Tyne Bridge from Newcastle. Some of the windows of its Weymann bodywork have been altered to flush fitting with rubber mountings, although this was not common within the batch. *David Wayman collection*

riverbank where some 100 years previously a young son of Gateshead, George Ridley, had had his leg amputated between a wagon wheel and the rail. Subsequently he was to be successful in making a living as a music-hall entertainer and composer of dialect songs, among them 'Blaydon Races'. Poor Geordie may not have been educated, but at least his doggerel tended to rhyme and scan.

Never mind Blaydon Races, you should have seen us gannin' up Gateshead High Street. You'd have had plenty of time. That Guy Arab was no streak, but eventually it reached the Sunderland Road End stop (1.2 miles). Here was the junction with the A184 road, where service 40 and others went left for a fairly level stretch, the 40 continuing by the shortest route available to Sunderland. Many service 40 journeys continued to (or made connections for) West Hartlepool.

A few more folk climbed aboard 1421, and three rings of the bell (unofficially) denoted a full standing load. Shortly the A1 forked right, taking other bus services, but 1421 continued ahead, as service 64 did, on the old road to Durham. The driver managed, in a while, to make a clutch-stop change up to third. There was no further acceleration, however, and soon he had to drop it back down to second. Mavis then made a profound statement initiating the following conversation, paraphrased and amplified for greater clarity.

"Eeh, this bus is goin' slow up this bank!"

"Oh Mavis, so you *do* notice things about buses! And d'you want me to tell you *why* it's going so slow?"

"No, but I think you will anyway."

"Right. Well, this is a heavy bus with a full load and it's not very powerful. The engine has a nominal output of 94bhp at 1,700rpm governed speed. Ah-huh, I know that because it says so in the Ian Allan *ABC of Buses and Coaches*. And yes, the unladen weight, which is given on the side of the bus, is 8.4.0, and that means eight tons, four hundredweight. Now let's see: 56 seated plus five standing plus a crew of two — that's 63 in all — with an official average of ten stones each — yes, I'm sure, because Alan Townsin said it in an article in *Buses Illustrated* — no, never mind who he is — that's 630 stone, divide it by eight and that's … (long pause for mental calculation) … 78¾cwt, or 3.18.3. Now, add that to the unladen weight and it's … er, 12.2.3, which is 242¾cwt, plus the weight of fluids which we don't know, but disregarding that figure it gives us a power-to-laden-weight ratio of, of, of … well, not very much."

"Keep showin' off, lad. You're curin' my insomnia better than any sleepin' pills."

Oh heavens, it was incredible how a lass could show such a lack of interest in these absorbing details. A lass, a lack and that smoggy upper saloon as a forum for debate on bus performance plus, among other travellers, the afternoon's sporting events at St James's Park. These latter discussions were liberally punctuated with blasphemous expressions and vulgar insults like "you frightful bounder", as well as sonorous oral emissions that were sweetly scented with the aroma of brewers' products. What an agreeable environment for a romantic journey home!

The chief cause for concern, however, was 1421's rate of progress up the confounded hill. At the section called Brunswick Street, where the gradient increased, the five-pot Gardner began to struggle. On this stretch, when it had been part of the Wrekenton tram route operated jointly until 1950 by the company cars of Gateshead & District and the municipal ones of Newcastle, there had been a descending speed limit of 8mph, with a liberal sprinkling of Board of Trade compulsory stops throughout the whole length of the hill.

Shortly beyond the junction where Split Crow Road (2.0 miles) branched left the grade eased somewhat, and 1421's Gardner was able to reach governed speed again. Then at the Old Cannon Inn (2.8 miles), on the section called Sodhouse Bank, it became steeper again, and the revs began to fall. There were other parts of the Northern system where a drop to first was frequently needed with well-laden heavyweight Guys, but was this going to be one more?

It sure was, for at about 7mph the change down was made, and 1421 just crawled until a change up was possible. At least two passengers wondered whether their gamble was going to pay off. That power-to-weight ratio for the heavyweight Guy, incidentally, worked out at 0.387bhp per cwt fully laden. The figure for a related company's lightweight 9.8-litre Leyland Titan PD2 56-seaters would have been 0.578. It's all theoretical stuff, of course, but perhaps interesting for comparison and contrast.

Once it was over the top, and faced with a gently falling gradient, the Guy was made to gallop. However, one's remembered impression is that these heavyweights had the 6.25:1 rear-axle ratio, which made the Arab — named after a speedy and tenacious breed of horse — a somewhat short-legged creature. Nevertheless, the Team Colliery Waggonway level crossing seemed to flash by, and before anyone realised it the bus had arrived in Wrekenton (3.9 miles, due there 10.42), 4-5min late, where it lost some of its load. This was where the weaving began, for it would turn left and right successively several times over the next three miles or so after an almost straight course from Pilgrim Street.

The gradients were now favourable. Top speed under power could not have been more than about 32-33mph, but those Northern drivers knew how to minimise loss of acceleration by using the clutch stop for fast changes up, and knocking the stick out for who knows how many extra miles per hour on the downhill stretches. Oh aye, veterans like old Wilkinson, Thorogood, Brocki, Carr, Carroll and Carlyon at Sunderland depot were experts. The doyen was steady Billy Urwin, and when he retired in the early 1960s he had piloted Northern buses more than a million miles — *accident-free*.

Bearing down on Springwell (5.3 miles, due 10.47), 1421 recouped about a minute. Its driver was economising on every ticking second, and there weren't many fare-payers left on board as the bus wove into Washington bus station (7.5 miles, due 10.55) about a couple of minutes down. More folk alighted here, fewer boarded, and 1421 zoomed off. Service 22 from Newcastle reached this point by a shorter route out of Gateshead, then shared the course of the 64 to Sunderland. Two 22s and a 64 per hour at not quite even intervals made up the basic Saturday co-ordinated service via Washington. At this juncture Boyfriend remarked that away to the south a little stood Washington Old Hall, mediæval home of the ancestors of the first President of the USA, adding: "I cannot tell a lie."

The significance of this remark was lost on Mavis.

But now came the final test of 1421. Strange batch, these 20 with Park Royal bodies; while most stated their unladen weight to be 8.1.0, at least Nos 1421, 1422 and 1424, all of Sunderland depot, claimed to be 3cwt heavier. Their comely body outline was obviously derived from the design of the London RT type, in which Park Royal had been so deeply involved. Along with that of a further 20 similar Arabs with stylish Weymann bodies, also built in 1952 and with an unladen weight of 7.18.1, their seating must have been among the most comfortable of any double-deck type that didn't profess to be a coach.

There were then two other batches of heavyweight 5LW-powered Guys in Northern's fleet, new in 1950, comprising eight Brush- and 11 Northern Coachbuilders-bodied specimens, unladen weights 8.0.0 and 7.18.0 respectively. Gateshead & District operated some identical Brush- and NCB-bodied Guys on its mountainous routes, along with some slightly lighter specimens bearing Park Royal bodies of earlier design.

Below: Representing 11 vehicles with Northern Coachbuilders bodywork built locally in Newcastle, a Guy Arab III in the Northern fleet lays over in dismal surroundings. The related Gateshead company had six similar buses, which were later acquired by Northern. All 17 had Northern's style of indicator layout, as shown here. *H. W. Peers*

Above: Another Guy Arab III 5LW batch of which identical examples could be seen in the Northern and Gateshead fleets comprised 17 with Brush bodies. Pictured here in Newcastle on a service operated jointly with that municipality is a dignified-looking 35, numerically the last of Gateshead's nine. They bore the registration numbers they would have had if delivered to Northern, although the destination aperture layout of all 17 was Gateshead's. Six of the batch ended up with Northern later. *J. Fozard*

Below: After the 59 heavyweight Guy double-deckers of 1950-2 (in addition to earlier, lighter types), in the years 1953-6 Northern acquired 81 medium- and lightweight 5LW Arab IVs (plus two later from Gateshead). This Metro-Cammell Orion-bodied example is the first of the 31 delivered in 1955, leaving Sunderland's Wearmouth Bridge followed by a Sunderland Corporation bus. *Alan B. Cross*

Above: In the writer's opinion the 5LW engine was more suitable for Northern's 134 Brush-bodied Guy Arab saloons of modified design, weighing some 6½ tons unladen, than in a heavy double-decker. This 38-seater was new in 1947. *J. Fozard*

Had the terrain of these companies been predominantly flat, such widespread use of the 5LW in hefty double-deckers would have been understandable. The Gardner 'five' may have been adequate for Northern's 6½-ton Guy Arab III saloons, totalling some 130, but with so many long — and even short — drags to negotiate, one can almost imagine harassed double-decker drivers muttering: "If only this **** old crate had another cylinder …" No, they didn't like them and would rather have had a rough 7.7-litre AEC Regent (all now withdrawn) or a smooth 9.8-litre Leyland Titan (a minority type, none of which was allocated to Sunderland depot).

The heavyweight Guys were considered to be reasonable pullers at low revs, but somewhat underpowered. It is obvious that Northern's affection for 5LW Guys arose from experience with wartime examples, many of which were not a great deal lighter than the later heavyweights. Moreover, there can be no doubt that, right up to the withdrawal in 1970 of the last of the subsequent, lighter Arab IVs, Guy buses had a high reputation for fuel economy and reliability.

But 1421 was now racing down to the level crossing and out into open country, with an immediate slowing for a 90° left turn followed within seconds by another to the right. Ah, but now there was a longish and straight run with a very slight falling tendency; 1421 just tore along at a breathtaking 33mph or so. Had Boyfriend possessed the gift of prophecy and intoned "One day all the land around here will be the site of a giant factory making motor cars with a Japanese name," the reply would most certainly have been,

"Don't talk daft, man." (But then, without the gift he'd have thought it daft himself.)

On and on thundered the Arab, clattering over another level crossing, but, sorry, no BR Standard '9F' loco hammering up to Consett from Tyne Dock with a 600-ton train of iron ore at this time of night. At the Three Horse Shoes (9.3 miles, due 11.02) no-one was interested in a thrilling adventure aboard 1421, now only about a minute behind schedule according to Timex. Next, inside the Sunderland County Borough boundary, it was to be hoped the bus didn't waken any sleeping bairns in the housing estate to the right. The road took a long and gentle curve rightwards, and, on a surface that could have done with a damned good ironing, 1421 hurtled past what was left of Hylton Castle with a roar enough to alarm the Cauld Lad o' Hylton on his nightly haunting of the eerie ruins.

Left a bit, up a bit, "Time it was widened here," then straight again on another gentle descent — this was the preamble to a slowing for sharply right, sharply up, sharply down and then sharply left on an adverse camber. So the bus came to Southwick (13 miles, due 11.13) near the tram terminus with the Tram Car Inn on the right. Too bad, last car from here had departed seven years previously. A few revellers got off, and the bus was now slightly ahead of time.

The mile along Southwick Road to the Wheat Sheaf junction seemed like nothing. Only about 0.7 mile to go now! Green-and-cream local municipal buses were heading for home. There was no slacking of the Guy's pace across Wearmouth Bridge. Next thing, two passengers were on the platform ready to leap off at the Town Hall (14.8 miles) as soon as 1421's speed allowed. The bus had made it from Southwick within seven minutes non-stop, and then hurried on to the bus station (due 11.23) with adjacent depot.

The two individuals' escapade was far from over, for now came a 250yd dash to where it was hoped the 49 would still be waiting. Rounding the corner, the sprinters were just in time … to see the bus pulling away. OK, so it would have to be the 11.30 after all. Well, it had been worth a try. The bus came in and commenced its final journey of the day, going only as far as the Sunderland District Omnibus Co's depot, which was on the route at Philadelphia (only about five miles south of Washington by the direct road). A navy-blue and white 1950 Roe-bodied Leyland Titan PD2, it was, No 235 in the company's 109-strong fleet, and full use was made of the 9.8-litre engine's capabilities. The path of service 49 was slightly indirect on leaving the town centre, adding 3min to the time allowed for direct routes along Durham Road.

Now Boyfriend was still thinking ahead. He knew that by the time they alighted at East Herrington (Beckwith Road) and he chivalrously walked Mavis home, the last bus on service 57 from Durham at 11.25, a Northern, would be almost due to leave

Houghton-le-Spring, three miles away. If, maybe, he could just hurry Mavis a bit and then test his own quarter-mile capabilities, he could make it to the junction of Durham Road and Thorney Close Road, another former tram terminus, to catch the inrushing bus. Better run in that direction, for if he did miss it he would be heading the right way for the rest of his three-mile walk home. Catching the bus would reduce it by nearly a mile.

Well, with Mavis seen safely indoors and hoping he wouldn't be hampered too much by his armour, which was glinting in the moonlight, Boyfriend whizzed to the arterial road. It was nearly 11.55, and the bus driver would likely pay scant regard to the scheduled time of midnight at East Herrington (Board Inn), about 0.6 mile before Boyfriend's planned embarking-point. Probably with sparks (if not smoke) flying from his steel heel tips — a literal attachment, those! — he clattered down the road and leaned against the bus stop post, lungs heaving like chapel-organ bellows.

Within less than a minute the Metro-Cammell Orion-bodied Guy Arab IV 5LW was braking for the stop, its crew probably wondering what senseless fool would want to get on their bus at that time of night. The near-mile was duly cut from Boyfriend's walk.

Well, it hadn't been a bad night, he mused as he got off the bus. It was going to be a pleasant walk home in the moonlight. And it would have been, if the clouds hadn't obscured the moon and the rain begun pouring down.

NB: Names of all females altered to protect the innocent — sorry, the author.

Left: Waterloo Place at noon on a Sunday, as here, was very different from the same location late on a Saturday night. Here at the spot where Mavis and Boyfriend saw their intended connection disappearing is a Sunderland District Omnibus 1950 Roe-bodied Leyland Titan PD2/1 of the same batch as the bus they did eventually catch. They had sprinted from opposite the Town Hall, visible above and to the right of the bus. *Roy Marshall*

Airport Transfers

JOHN HOWIE looks at those operators and vehicles — normally former PSVs pensioned off by their original owners — which over three decades have provided essential logistical support at Gatwick Airport.

A longside the express services, local buses and hotel, car-park and car-hire courtesy coaches which ply the roads around Gatwick Airport there runs a fleet of buses which rarely stray beyond the airport boundary. Some, in fact, have such restricted use that they do not carry registration plates. Their use can be categorised as follows:

- Airside — transporting passengers or aircrew between aircraft and terminal building within the Customs-controlled zone
- Public/staff car parking — linking public car parks with terminals and transporting staff between staff car parks and various on-airport sites and terminals

From their introduction in 1973 until the turn of the century most of these services were provided by second-hand buses, many of which had already seen considerable previous use, but a change of policy in 2000 saw their replacement by new equipment. This narrative restricts itself mainly to the nature and deployment of these former PSVs but also includes references to some other vehicles which from time to time were used to supplement them.

First a few key facts about Gatwick Airport, to demonstrate its development over the period:

	1973	1988	2000
Terminals	1	2	2
Passengers	5.8 million	15.2 million	30.4 million
Employees	10,000	18,000	27,000
Number of car-park bus-transfer services			
Public	Nil	2	4
Staff	Nil	1	3

As can be seen, there are considerable numbers of people who require transporting every day.

Initially all facilities at the airport were sufficiently compact to make walking the most practical method of moving about. However, expansion not only meant that aeroplanes had to be parked away from the terminal, but land use requirements caused non-critical activities (such as car parking) to be moved to more distant locations. The first instance of this occurred in April 1975, when the main entrance and car parks were moved from the A23 London–Brighton road to the east of the railway, necessitating an internal car-park bus service. Later, a similar service was required for staff as their car-park sites were developed for commercial use; hence these facilities gradually became more remote from the terminal.

The opening of the North Terminal in March 1988 (from which date the original building was re-designated the South Terminal) saw the introduction of a complementary set of services for staff and public, with a consequent need for additional vehicles. Similarly, physical expansion due to increased numbers of flights and passengers meant that the distance from terminal to plane became impractical to walk. The introduction of piers and the rail shuttle met some of the demand, but there was still a requirement for many aircraft to be loaded some distance away, and this generated a need for airside vehicles.

The accompanying schedule summarises all former PSVs known to have operated at Gatwick. It should be noted that additionally there were similar vehicles engaged on these activities (particularly those of British Airways) which have been excluded, as they were purchased new. However, to avoid meaningless gaps, a number are included which had not technically seen prior non-airport use (as they originated with British Airways), as are a few vehicles new to National Car Parks.

Airside transfers

Responsibility for the transfer of passengers to and from aircraft rests with the airlines, but they traditionally contract handling agents to perform all ground-based activities (check-in, baggage transfer, baggage reclaim, aircraft tugs and transport), as there are economies of scale in collective provision.

Gatwick buses — summary of main vehicle types

Gatwick Handling Ltd, 1973-94 (airside passenger and crew transfers)
6	AEC Merlin/Strachans	ex London Transport (MBS class)
3	AEC Swift/MCW	ex London Country (SM class)
2	AEC Swift/MCW	ex London Transport (SMS class)
11	AEC Merlin/MCW	ex London Country (MBS class)
3	AEC Merlin/MCW	ex London Transport (MBS class)
27	Leyland National	ex National Bus (Crosville, Trent, Devon General etc)

British Caledonian Airways, 1977-87 (airside passenger transfers, airside/landside crew transfers)
14	AEC Merlin/MCW	ex London Transport (MBS class)
7	Leyland National	ex London Country (LN class)
2*	Bristol LHS/ECW	ex Southern Vectis/London Transport (BS class)
2*	Bristol RELL/ECW	ex Hants & Dorset

* may have been more

British Airways, 1987-9 (airside passenger transfers, airside/landside crew transfers)
6	AEC Merlin/MCW	ex British Caledonian
4	Leyland National	ex British Caledonian
5	Leyland National	ex London Transport (LS class)

British Airtours, 1977-83 (airside passenger and crew transfers)
3	AEC Merlin/MCW	ex London Transport (MBS class)
2	Leyland National	ex British Airways

KF Cars, 1979-91 (airside crew transfers and staff car parks)
2	AEC Swift/MCW	ex London Country (SM class)
6	Metro-Scania	ex Ivy, Huddersfield
8	Leyland National	ex London Transport (LS class)/Midland Red and others

Glynglen, 1989-92 (airside passenger and crew transfers)
9	Leyland National	ex London Transport (LS class)

National Car Parks, 1979-89 (public car parks)
4	AEC Swift/MCW	ex London Country (SM class)
8	Leyland National	new
1	Shelvoke & Drewry/Reeve-Burgess	demonstrator

Capital Coaches, 1992-2000 (airside passenger and crew transfers)
30	Leyland National	ex other airport operators
11*	DAF SB220/Hispano	ex Trans Island Bus Service, Singapore

* exact number not confirmed

NB: list excludes (with a few exceptions) vehicles not previously operated as PSVs

At Gatwick during the latter part of the 20th century these agents were British Caledonian (BCal), British Airways (BA), Gatwick Handling (GHL) — which was initially known as Airline Express and was originally a consortium of Dan-Air and Laker Airways —and Ogden Allied. Airport policy restricted the number of handling agents; hence all engaged in third-party work for other airlines as well as servicing their own aircraft fleets.

Prior to 1973 passenger numbers were such that most could walk to and from the aircraft, and the vehicle requirement was met by British Airways'

transferring vehicles from Heathrow or (in the case of BCal) using a small number of articulated units. There was, also, the occasional purchase of old coaches. However, the six ex-London Transport Strachans-bodied AEC Merlins delivered to GHL in June 1973 were the forerunners of approximately 150 former PSVs which would traverse the ever-expanding Gatwick concrete over the next 27 years. The choice of vehicle type was a natural one, given the requirement to carry the maximum number of people over a short distance, as they were originally designed for high-capacity Red Arrow routes. Their

Left: The Merlins later received Gatwick Handling white, black and red livery, as demonstrated by this vehicle on the airport perimeter road. *J. Chisholm*

replacements (MBS, SM and SMS types) were to a similar specification, while the third generation (Leyland Nationals) were even more suitable, as their modular construction facilitated rearrangement of seating and the insertion of an additional offside door, although in practice few vehicles were modified to this extent.

Gatwick Handling

The six initial Merlins soon proved inadequate to cope with passenger growth, and from 1976 these were supplemented by a further 19 rear-engined AECs from the MBS, SM and SMS classes in the fleets of London Transport or London Country. These vehicles were re-seated to 25 and carried internal GH 'registrations' directly related to their previous fleet number; thus, for example, the former SM501 became GH 501. The original Merlins (which had borne numbers GH 171-6) became increasingly dilapidated and ceased to be used around 1979. Five passed to dealer Cranes & Commercials at Lasham, the sixth (JLA 63D)

remaining on the airport in a damaged condition as the property of KF Cars, of which more anon.

By 1984 the later AECs were also well past their best, and the majority passed to Allco for scrapping (one notable escapee being DPD 502J, which joined Basil Williams' Southern Motorways fleet). Their replacements were Leyland Nationals, of which many quality examples were appearing on the second-hand market, and a total of 27 arrived from four National Bus Company fleets — Crosville, Devon General, Trent and Bristol. These were prepared by the engineers at Alder Valley and configured with either 21 coach seats (for crew transfer) or 17 bus seats (for passenger use), in which layout it was possible to accommodate up to 100 people on one vehicle — albeit with a bit of a squeeze! Again, airport internal identities were carried, but these gave no clue as to former owner. However, this could often be deduced from tell-tale markings on individual vehicles, such as the retention of interior fleet numbers, depot codes and the like. A 28th National (KBY 792P) was not, strictly speaking, a former PSV, having been delivered new to British Airways and acquired in 1983 with perimeter seating for 17.

GHL's basic livery was a combination of red, white and black, the exact application changing over time and differing between individual vehicles.

From 1992 some of the airside-transfer business, including a number of vehicles, passed to Capital Coaches; remaining vehicles saw a further two years' use before being sold. Amazingly, in 1994, some re-entered front-line public passenger service with GM Buses South, including the very early production model (WFM 801K) that had been new to Crosville. It would appear that airport duties were not too onerous on the mechanical components, as there are neither hills nor frequent stops; hence the vehicles had not aged significantly during their sojourn at Gatwick.

Above: A line-up of GHL vehicles, all carrying 'airport registrations' which relate directly to their previous London Transport or London Country fleet numbers. *John Howie*

Left: This Leyland National was one of a number of ex-National Bus Company examples which were adapted for airport use by Alder Valley Engineering. This particular vehicle was originally Crosville WFM 823L. It later passed to Capital Coaches for continued use at Gatwick. *P. Snell*

Right: GH 303 parked beside Gatwick Handling's training Comet. Note how the aircraft's wings have been 'clipped' in the interests of safety and stability. *P. Snell*

British Caledonian

Passenger growth also required that British Caledonian build up a vehicle fleet for both passenger and crew transfers. Like GHL it made good use of former London Transport Merlins, and 14 were purchased between 1976 and 1983. As some of their duties were on public roads original registrations were carried on all vehicles, although probably only one or two were actually taxed, the others remaining exclusively airside. Again, Leyland Nationals were found to be ideal successors, and seven of the original L-registered examples arrived from London Country in 1981, although no Merlins were withdrawn. Also in operation at this date were a number of vehicles of Bristol/ECW manufacture; at least two RELL buses (ex Hants & Dorset) and two LHs (ex-Southern Vectis or London Transport) were used on crew-transfer duties, and there may have been additional examples.

The basic fleet was still complete when BCal merged with British Airways in December 1987, and a significant number of vehicles transferred to the new airline. The majority of those that did not found a new home at Birmingham Airport.

British Airways

British Airways' buses and coaches were generally purchased new from manufacturers and thus, having no previous PSV operator, fall outside the scope of this article. However, the acquisition in 1987 of BCal resulted in the transfer of a number of Merlins and Leyland Nationals to accommodate the additional passengers. These vehicles were given BA fleet numbers BU6019-24 (Merlins) and BU6001 etc (Nationals). Most of the Nationals were repainted into BA blue, but only one (or possibly two) of the AECs received the new colours. Replaced by new vehicles and by transfers from Heathrow, the AECs had all left by June 1989, followed by the Nationals in late 1991. Many saw further airport use, principally at Dublin, Belfast (Harbour) or Edinburgh.

British Airtours

This branch of British Airways commenced operations from Gatwick, with a small fleet of Boeing 707 aircraft, in 1977. Passengers were transported in three ex-London Transport Merlins with MCW bodies until 1983, after which vehicles from the main BA fleet were introduced.

Left: A British Caledonian ex-London Transport Merlin, with the shuttle car to the South Terminal Satellite passing overhead in the background.
John Howie

Right: British Caledonian used at least two Bristol LHs for crew-transfer duties. This ECW-bodied LHS was new to London Transport.
J. Chisholm

Ogden Allied

In 1989 a fourth handling agent was introduced, to provide additional competition. The business was run as Ogden Allied, but the airside buses (ex-London Transport Nationals) were provided by Glynglen (a company registered in North Finchley) and were identified by a Tristar reference. Numbers were between 1 and 10 with the missing ones operating at Stansted. The initial, all-black livery proved difficult to see at night and was modified by the addition of yellow and other lighter colours. A couple of the vehicles were withdrawn in 1991, but the remainder passed to Capital in March 1992, when the transfer of airside passengers was reorganised.

Capital Coaches

Capital had a presence at Gatwick from the 1970s, as it provided a mix of hotel courtesy coaches and vehicles for crew transfers and car-park transfers, the last-named on behalf of National Car Parks, an associated company. However, from March 1992 a reorganisation of terminal-to-aircraft transfers resulted in its undertaking the work previously performed by GHL and Ogden Allied; at this time it acquired the Tristar and GHL Nationals, which were given CAP xx identification and painted in a red/white livery. Most were replaced in November 1996 by similar vehicles formerly used by Whyte's (another associated company) at Heathrow (some of which were thus technically not former PSVs). Confusingly, they were given CAP numbers in the same series as their predecessors, making identification difficult, although many of the later examples remained in Whyte's yellow or blue. They did not last long at Gatwick, and the final examples departed as part of a further reorganisation in April 2000. Many (if not all) of the 1996 disposals were

via Nash of Weybridge, a dealer specialising in Nationals. Some reappeared locally, notably with Frimley Coaches of Aldershot, Edward Thomas of West Ewell and Thames Valley Training, and one even migrated north to serve with Melvin of Dyce. To supplement the Nationals a fleet of Hispano-bodied DAFs was imported from Singapore and brought into use from April 1997. Again, these were allocated CAP numbers, but some were also given G-prefix registrations to allow their use on crew-transfer and staff car-park services. They were ideal for servicing smaller aircraft, but fixed seats made them less suitable for larger loads. All survived until April 2000, when yet another reorganisation necessitated their replacement by new vehicles. Perhaps surprisingly, many were sold for PSV use.

Car-park services

Continuing growth displaced both passenger and public car parking to locations distant from the terminals, the resultant transfer service being provided initially by National Car Parks vehicles (for the public) and KF Cars (for staff). The latter also undertook a small amount of airside work and, for at least some of the time, provided drivers for the GHL fleet.

KF Cars

KF Cars was a private company owned by Ken Ffolkes — hence the KF Cars name — which began operations at Gatwick in 1979, initially transferring airline crews to local hotels. The vehicles used for this purpose were mainly Duple-bodied Fords and are outside the scope of this article. However, in 1980 KF acquired an ex-London Country SM-class AEC Swift and a similar bus from the airport NCP fleet. These vehicles were used for the odd airside contract, but major expansion

occurred in 1988, when a fleet of six Metro-Scanias, originally with Newport Borough Council, was acquired from Ivy of Huddersfield. Some of these were used on the staff car-park contract, whilst others (bearing KFC x numbers) remained airside for crew transfers. However, their sojourn at Gatwick proved short, and all had gone by June 1989. Replacements were the by now ubiquitous Leyland Nationals, once in the fleets of London Transport or Midland Red. Bearing internal identification KFC 1-8, these remained until early 1991; some then transferred to Stansted Airport, whilst the rest went to Yorkshire dealers for scrap.

NCP

As stated earlier, operations commenced in 1975 with the opening of the large surface long-term car park east of the London–Brighton railway. Most of the vehicles were new Duple- or Plaxton-bodied Fords, but four ex-London Country SM-class AECs arrived in 1979. Also worthy of note is the deployment of the unique Shelvoke & Drewry Airport Bus, which, incidentally, was used to carry the Royal welcoming party on the arrival of the Pope in 1982. The fleet was completely renewed by the arrival of eight new Leyland Nationals in 1982/3; one SM had already passed to KF Cars, but the others went for scrap. In 1989 contractual arrangements changed, necessitating the purchase of a new fleet, the Nationals moving to either Stansted or Heathrow. Only one escaped further airport duties, appearing with Ashford Luxury of Bedfont.

Into the 21st century

Inevitably, revised policies and commercial pressures required the provision of more suitable and modern vehicles; hence from 2000 passengers and visitors at Gatwick were no longer transported in superannuated buses. Airside transfers are now performed not by other people's cast-offs but by Cobuses (Cobi?); the public are transported to/from car parks in the latest Wrightbus-bodied Scanias, while airport staff have forsaken a journey in a Metro-Scania in favour of travelling by gas power in a DAF/East Lancs Myllennium.

eft: New to Newport **orporation** but acquired **om** Ivy, Huddersfield, this **etro-Scania** worked for **F Cars** for six months in **arly** 1989. It is pictured at **e** end of its short airport **fe,** awaiting collection for **crap.** Note the obligatory **oof-mounted** orange **eacon.** *John Howie*

elow left: An ex-London **ountry** SM-class AEC Swift **sed** by NCP, parked **djacent** to the long-term **ir** park at Gatwick in 1981. *ewart J. Brown*

Above: In 1982/3 NCP bought eight new Leyland Nationals to replace the SM-type Swifts. This would be the only one to escape the airport for further use, being sold in 1989 to Ashford Luxury. *John Howie*

Left: The unique Shelvoke & Drewry Airport Bus spent some of 1982 working for NCP at Gatwick. *John Howie*

Below: Present-day staff transport is represented by this East Lancs Myllennium-bodied DAF SB220, running on LPG and operated by Airlinks between car parks and the terminals. *John Howie*

The Last Sunday Bus to Potter Heigham

All photographs by the authc

In the midst of tangled emotions, with reminiscences from days long gone and recent attacks on the territory, a mixture of medium success and total failure, ROBERT E. JOWITT tackles, with his habitual side-tracking but in perhaps his most lyrical even if most convoluted essay ever, the byways of East Anglian bus operations.

In the summer of the year of grace 2004 I had a tryst, on a Thursday, to meet a beautiful foreign lady, of whom I do not care to divulge more than the fact her name begins with M. The original intention was for me to meet her at Heathrow, but this proved to be at too unholy an hour for me to contemplate, so the next idea was for me to meet her at Brockenhurst, Hants, New Forest (Southern Region — as I must forever think of it), whence we could wander in the woods; but, anyway, in the way of volatile foreign ladies, she took it into her head to catch the next plane on from Heathrow to Edinburgh, to inspect something on the fringe, whither I could not follow, not least because I could not afford to fly to the Athens of the North.

Accordingly we reached a compromise.

My third child, aged 13, had been offered as a birthday present by his Godmother a holiday at a Christian youth camp in the wilds of Norfolk, starting on the Saturday of the same week. As it seemed my duty to convey him thither — and funking the M25 from the South Coast — I elected to undertake this task by train rather than by car, especially as the Norfolk Christians were prepared to meet such contingencies by collecting train-delivered children at Wymondham (pronounced 'Wyndham', as in John and *Triffids*), for I could then rearrange the tryst with M, now due to head south from Edinburgh, to take place in Norwich, and then, with M, to make an exploration by bus and by boat of Norwich and the Norfolk Broads.

M and I, may I add, had already suffered the intransigencies of East Anglian bus operations, and in this previous case on her behalf (though not without my own problems in this area, as I shall shortly reveal), so I felt she might well suffer further in the same vein.

At this juncture I should add that East Anglian bus operations are far beyond my usual range of study of such matters as in Paris or Portugal or even Portsmouth, and accordingly I must render a brief summary of my earlier experiences (such as they were) — including those (such as they weren't) with M — in this zone …

In 1965 I set out on a serious study of windmills in East Anglia. In this the only buses which caught my attention were those elderly jewels of Mulleys at Ixworth, which, though undoubtedly already familiar to the early *cognoscenti* of the Historic Commercial Vehicle Club, came to me as a completely unexpected delight amidst sheep-filled fields. The rest of the buses, so far as I bothered to discern them at all, were ordinary Eastern Counties or Eastern National or whatever they may have been, just Tilling-common-or-garden-Bristol-ECW Lodekkas or the rest, exactly like Hants & Dorset at home, not worth a second glance …

My second and serious glance was a quarter-of-a-century later …

In the early 1990s, with a sister-in-law on the fringes of Sudbury and her Nth wedding-anniversary party, I achieved brief attacks on the bus stations in said Sudbury and Colchester, and on the streets of Colchester besides. Obviously,

Above: First East Anglian encounter — 40 years ago, in July 1965. With a bosky background a couple of Mulley's jewels — a Regent and a Titan — linger in the yard at Ixworth.

Left: Sudbury bus station, February 1991 — another encounter for author's future reference. On the left is a Rule's of Boxford Leyland Leopard/Plaxton Supreme, in the centre a Theobald's of Long Melford 1978 Bedford YMT/Supreme, and on the right a Hedingham Omnibus Iveco/Carlyle.

Left: Colchester Borough Transport received 36 ECW-bodied Atlanteans — a combination relatively unusual outside NBC. This one is seen in February 1991.

Above right: The charm of an Atlantean rear end, commonplace when this photograph was taken in 1991 but soon to become a rare sight.

Below right: In 1991 Colchester operated Leyland Lynxes. One loads in the High Street.

Right: A Colchester Olympian shelters under the multi-storey car park — since demolished — which for three decades towered over the bus station.

Left: Seen from the vantage-point of the bus station car park, a Colchester Atlantean arrives on a winter's day.

with my usual almost total ignorance of what I am trying to photograph, save only if it looks antique — or, be it anything else, if there is a pretty girl in front of it, when I will shoot it and girl, regardless — I had little idea whether I was catching something of the relicts of Colchester Corporation Transport or some new post-deregulation delights; but — a dozen or so years later, upon printing for the first time these negatives, for the sake of my esteemed readers — I discover that Colchester Borough Transport had some interesting double-deckers which boasted a top deck which looks like ECW VR style while the rear-end rump is plainly Leyland Atlantean, even if with a touch of added ventilators. I cannot recall paying much attention to this phenomenon at the time, and may not even have been aware *then* of what *now* appears unusual and even meritorious. At all events, if belatedly, I think I can congratulate myself on having shot the creatures… and an Eastern National Leyland National (sounds well patriotic, doesn't it?) or two — as well as the girls …

I now move on a decade to another anniversary party, this time with what — or whom — must alas (and none of my wishing) be described as *ex*-sister-in-law, by now removed to the village of Glemsford, some miles out of Sudbury. With this visit impending, and proposing to approach same by public transport (for the same non-M25 reasons indicated earlier in these pages), I go to some trouble to bother my excellent friend and great authority on East Anglian transport, the renowned Ian Cowley, to despatch me a bus timetable for the relevant area. Thus armed, with four children and estranged wife (and under such circumstances the M25 journey from Portsmouth in Maestro would hardly have been bearable, would it?) and several trains culminating in a very exciting ride on a very ancient DMU from Marks Tey, we arrive in Sudbury.

Then:

Estranged Wife, to the world at large, if not REJ in particular: 'Why isn't there a taxi here at the station?'

REJ: 'The bus station is only five minutes' walk, and I have the times of the buses …'

EW: 'There'll be a taxi in the town …'

Three minutes beyond the bus station there is indeed a taxi rank, but:

Taxi-driver: 'No, this isn't a taxi rank any more, I'm just here 'cos it's my dinner break. There's a taxi rank up there …' He points vaguely northeast.

EW, angrily: 'All we want is to go to Glemsford!'

'Or back home,' I mutter to myself.

Taxi-driver: 'Up there!' over sandwich, vaguely again, but this time more crossly, northeast.

Up there, northeast, is empty. I wave Ian Cowley's timetable, suggestively …

The bus, I seem to recall, was a VR, or maybe an ex-London DMS, possibly one of Chambers' — and I could never see these without thinking of *pots* — but I was, in such situation, in no mind to note its details let alone to photograph it, though nevertheless I and two of the children made the most of its upper deck and appreciated its qualities on the passage to Glemsford while E. W. and the other two remained below.

The passage back to Sudbury, a couple of days later, was, so far as I remember, on a hideous single-deck (Chambers? *Pots?*) but tranquil, and then another choice DMU to Marks Tey … and onwards …

And the next time it wasn't such a nice DMU, only a couple of years later, early March 2004, but M and I had to use it anyway, modernised though the service was …

M and I had first met, quite by chance but romantically of course, on a Virgin train south of Oxford in December 2003 and subsequently, deliberately, several times, including at the King Alfred 1 January Running Day in Winchester and again in London, where I met two of her temporarily immigrated sons and deplored the decline of RMs and the shocking, alien sight of the replacing flammable bendy-buses (not that any actually burst into flame in my presence) and again in March, before her return to foreign parts (not, alas, to return to British shores until August), to trail to East Anglia, where one of these sons was now working on a farm in a place called, according to her, Bradfield Combust, where she and I must visit him to bid farewell. I naturally revolted at this — not, I hasten to add, at the idea of the meeting but at the name of the rendezvous … 'It sounds like some patent manure … or an atom bomb …' The Ordnance Survey proved me wrong, and Bradfield Combust proved to exist between Sudbury and Bury St Edmunds, so I had to crawl with apologies and accept the situation, and ex-sister-in-law generously promised to welcome M and me after our foray to patent manure and atom bomb, assuring us that plenty of buses served the route to Compost (no … whatever …) from Sudbury. I had in the meantime lost Ian Cowley's timetable, which anyway would have proved out of date …

Examination of a very battered timetable on the wall of Sudbury bus station proved that buses now, whatever they may have done before, avoided Bradfield Combust. We could walk on a mile from the nearest point of bus-route contact to the tavern adjacent to M's child's farm, where we intended to meet him. Instead we took ourselves a couple of hundred yards northeast, up there, and this time a taxi was apparent. The tavern at Bradfield Combust displayed inability to open for another hour or so, thus the same taxi conveyed us — me and M and M's son — a couple of miles further north to another tavern. In the total absence of the prospect of any more buses that night, dear ex-sister-in-law plus car came to the rescue, supped with us, dumped child thereafter at Combust and, the following morning, M and me at Sudbury station …

Regardless of these experiences, when this next tryst with M loomed on the horizon, I resolved once again to chance our luck to the tender world of public-service buses … But this, I must add, was not without some prior research. Let me here explain that whatever M's views on the matter as a foreigner ignorant of the rarer passages of English literature, I as a lifelong devotee of Arthur Ransome felt bound to make the most of a chance to explore *Coot Club* country … and with this purview in mind I tackled the Norwich Tourist Information Office on the phone and dug into an already outdated edition of the *Great British Bus Timetable* …

I suspect, with hindsight, that the charming girl in the Tourist Information Office was not aware of the very existence of PSV operations in the Norwich area. But, bless her, she did her best … and was quite convinced that if we wanted a bus from Norwich direct to Potter Heigham it must be on a Sunday, on a 718, and starting from Anglia Square … or, if we chose to travel to Potter Heigham on a weekday, we must travel half over Norfolk first. This latter opinion, I must admit, more or less tallied with my own conclusions from the derelict GBBT.

With Anglia Square in my mind I accordingly dropped my precious child at Wymondham and on the next train from there foregathered rejoicing with precious M's journey south from Edinburgh.

There are several ex-tramway-ornamented streets of Victorian villas leading out from the centre of Norwich, many of such villas now given over to B&B, and on one of these, bidden by the tourist guide book, M and I, by taxi, descended. Madame B&B insisted on Chistian names, not a habit I willingly accept, and while I forget what hers was, Sylvia or Sandra, I established her in my mind as Mrs Scarlet, because for all the four breakfasts we enjoyed she attended in a letterbox-red dress. Either, I concluded, she had several identical dresses, or else a very efficient washing machine. Her husband, I first of all believed, was an ex-military man, Colonel Mustard, due to his precision but subsequently I decided his mincing steps with delivery of bacon and sausage and fried egg were more likely a product of stage or, perchance, ballet.

Naturally I never solved these little mysteries, but

must admit to a moment of great delight when fastidious Mrs S in an exuberant gesture of breaking-fast bonhomie swept my coffee pot off the table onto the floor; 'Oh, oh, I've never done that before!' exclaimed she over the grand mess, 'but thank goodness the carpet's washable!' I expect the cleaning fell to the lot of the chambermaid, a splendid lady who, with seductive smiles at male guests, struggled against the oppression of her task by tackling it barefooted and with a transistor blasting Radio Norwich in her laundry basket.

Be these residential details as they may, the Vic villa was well served, like several other ex-tram routes, by FirstBus boxes, generally and give-or-take and unless-too-late-at-night, at ten-minute or twelve-minute intervals … though I must admit that more than once an over-long acquaintance with the nearest vomit-stained Adshel caused us to succumb to a passing taxi …

Never mind that; on the Sunday morn a FirstBus box hove into view, and M and I boarded; and I, all innocent, said: 'Two to Anglia Square, please.'

So, driver, entirely polite (and with what I believe to be a Norfolk accent): 'I'm not going to Anglia Square. Anglia Square's out. Road works. They only just told us!'

REJ: 'We want to catch the bus from Anglia Square to Potter Heigham, so what shall we do?'

Driver: 'You can catch it at Castle Meadow. I'm going there, and all the buses out of Norwich go there.'

He was right, and so far as I am concerned Castle Meadow had it all, every bus route; Anglia Square was but a flip or glip in the eye of that charming girl's computer. Nevertheless Castle Meadow produced its own problems. Among multitudinous bus stops, the one which boasted the magic number '718' had the name 'Potter Heigham' taped over! Sunday morning in Castle Meadow is not the best time to make enquiries, but a redoubtable FirstBus Inspectress — 'I used to be a driver' — did her best with my problems. 'Sunday buses to Potter Heigham … oh, they're being taken off … they're not ours … they may have been taken off already …', but after lengthy discussion in this vein an anonymous white bus hove into view at a different stop — anonymous, that is (for I was too flustered to see if it boasted any legal lettering, and it certainly bore no other proof of identity), save for

a piece of cardboard stuck in the windscreen proclaiming '718'.

'Are you going to Potter Heigham?'

'Yes.'

'Can we get on here?' Even to my eyes, so far not well-tutored in Norwich Geography, it seemed to be facing the wrong way.

'Yes.'

'Okay. Two to Potter Heigham.'

The driver carefully studied his fare chart, or, so far as I could see, the section of it dealing with Potter Heigham to Great Yarmouth, and concluded '£2 each,' again with a charming Norfolk accent. As a resident of the Isle of Wight I am well used to exorbitant fares, and this seemed to me very reasonable, whether or not it was correct, so I laid out £4 and received one ticket — I honestly can't remember if M pulled off a second — inscribed '£2' and 'CONC/SGL' and 'ROYALL', which title seems to me to agree, upon subsequent consultation, with the Norfolk County Council transport map (*q.v.* hereinafter) … and made enquiries about the prospects of a return journey …

The bus, anonymous or not, appeared to me extremely modern — not at all the derelict specimen you might expect on rural Sunday services — with little tiny headlights like illustrations in *National Geographic* of microscopic photos of insects' eyes, and of the type which might grovel in the gutter for wheelchairs and perambulators, and we set off on a grand tour of Norwich and back to the other side of Castle Meadow to another, different stop, where, had I but seen before, the magic name 'Potter Heigham' had been re-established.

'But it's coming off next weekend …'

Meanwhile we headed out in more or less direct line for Wroxham. The few senior citizens who boarded and then elapsed in Norwich suburbs were far too spritely for wheelchairs, and the only pushchair, somewhere beyond Horning, was heaved on with an abandon which would have served in Bristol L5G days.

At Potter Heigham the driver said to me: 'What you asked in Norwich, what I said I wasn't doing … yes, I am — I'm coming back on the 17.54 through Potter. This Sunday, anyways.'

'So if we don't go round by Great Yarmouth, like we would if you weren't,' said I, 'we'll see you here.'

A bus/boat voyage from Potter Heigham, however-much Ransome *déjà vu*, has no place in these pages, but I dare add that to Richard Chisnell, once upon a time a family stalwart in the activities of King Alfred Motor Services, Winchester, and then, bereft, becoming famous upon other pursuits such as adjudication on the public lavatories of Great Britain, those at P H should rate high on his blacklist … and we were back on the other side of the road at 17.54.

'What did I charge you on the way out? My ticket machine's broken.'

'£2 each. I used to drive PSV in Herefordshire — I had a ticket-machine like that.'

£4 in the sandwich box.

'But are they really taking this service off next weekend? For goodness sake,' politely, 'I don't want to bring a car here, I want to travel by bus, but … *how can I?*

Anyway on Monday, barring FirstBus box or a couple of taxis, we walked … the Market, the Art Nouveau Arcade, the Castle, the Cathedral, etc, and various public houses, and M then decided she was tired out and would retire to Mrs Scarlet, and, if I so wished, leave me to my own devices … or, as it so happened, the bus rush-hour in Castle Meadow.

For this I was in truth but ill-equipped. With increasing age and idleness I had more or less abandoned the notions of b&w bus photography, especially with the thought of several thousand b&w negs which I had not yet printed (as above, *e.g.* in Colchester) but I had brought on this excursion an elderly Zenith. I had tried this out already, noted that it would work only on the set shutter speed

(unknown), but it had sounded all-right on a Hippie bus (ex-Ribble mini-Mercedes) in the charge, in Newport, IoW, of a damsel with possibly the most divine form it has ever been my lot to behold. These test-shots, thus committed (as has now become my practice) to Hocus-Pocus-Instant-Color-Prints, had not been returned when I sallied forth with said Zenith to risk the fray of Norwich, but I wasn't seriously interested in photographing a lot of FirstBus boxes anyway, or any buses at all, so I would just risk derelict Zenith …

I must admit that even though what passed before my eyes was to me mostly unknown if possibly relatively ancient by today's standard biscuit boxes — mostly FirstBus Dennis Darts collected second-hand, as it were, from other FirstBus operations in post-deregulation chaos and transmogrifications of same in which I had little interest and less ability to comprehend — there were several more desirable specimens, and I must quote the slightly charming single-deckers with Irish registration plates which, so I am told afterwards, are ex-London Dennis Darts with Wrights of Ballymena bodies, bought by their original owner to replace (how cruel!) the RMs on routes 28/31. Then also in the FirstBus fleet were some seriously battered double-deckers with a charisma I have recognised elsewhere, perhaps in Edinburgh or even the IoW. And, not least, a Leyland Olympian/ECW, which, though plainly a rural or

pirate non-First and of extreme antiquity by its number-plate (actually ex-London Transport L75 of 1986 — one in the last batch of same ordered by LT) features by presumably sheer ignorance on the part of the compilers as the superstar on the front page of the latest Tourist Council map, which I have just acquired (it now being Monday), of PSV routes in Norwich and all East Anglia …

And with this and the other (if debatably charming) gems around me I naturally fall back into my usual practice of adding the youthful female elements of the population to my efforts. We are now, speaking fashion-wise, in the era of the midriff, as even the most casual observer, even if not interested in girls (or buses), can hardly fail to observe. The midriff displays a degree of exposure which might in some quarters well be conceived as wanton coupled to either the tiniest mini-skirt, and this usually with cowboy boots some way below, or else with very low-slung jeans — so low-slung, indeed, that the beholder must wonder how they stay where they are bidden — with the overall effect, save in a few rare cases of extreme slimness, that such exposition had better been eschewed. Nevertheless, given my artistic reputation, I cannot ignore it …

Perhaps with such diversions I don't study my newly acquired map enough to see what it says about the 54. On Tuesday we are back in Castle Meadow, and a 54 is what we want. I hadn't quite clicked it was a First — I am looking eagerly at the Olympian on the same timing — but M screams, correctly (Heavens, how much I, as authority on the subject, must blush!): 'Look! 54!' So we board the First box.

REJ: 'Is this going to Horning?'

'Yes.' Driver change, and, *sotto voce*, 'She ain't pulling well uphill …' in a Norfolk accent.

The ticket in my possession now suggests £4.20 return, but was this really for both M and me? Lack of ink on the machine and lack of memory prevail …

She (the bus) manages, despite threatened weakness, passably heartily, box though she may be, the only serious gradient from the river to the plains and then on in a series of right-angles through bungaloid villages to Wroxham and then via Sunday's route to Horning.

Before we embark on a river trip we think about lunch and halt at the Post Office.

The Post Office produces, apart from such fare as you might expect, a book of ancient photos of Norwich trams (from which, I readily admit, any conclusions I may have drawn above on this subject are based), but, not wishing to risk it to the hazards of another river-boat cruise, I leave this tome in the PO, to be collected later.

The next river-boat cruise is surely all that Ransome would hate, but in practical terms all I can achieve to visit the scenes of *Coot Club* and *The Big Six*. It is actually a screw-driven catamaran, but in fancy dress clad as a Mississippi stern-wheeler, the stern-wheel turning merely by means of current,

if any, and dressed moreover in a paddle-box such as surely no stern-wheeler (only side-wheelers!) ever possessed … and rather over full with a coach party.

Some days later I had to thrust M onto a South West Train at Southampton, in possibly or maybe all-too-probably a terminal farewell, and so then I thought, with writing of East Anglia already in my mind, that I would chase up that previous item from the pages of *Buses Yearbook*, namely the articulated buses which, in Southampton, I had never seen save at night and unphotographically.

With two or three spectacular midriffs on the way (to add to fashion photos I had been doing in Soton for 30 years, some of them even reaching *Buses Yearbook*, although the buses now were nearly all First boxes no different, for all I could tell, from those I had just seen in Norwich) I sought the place I thought the articulateds should be, only to find a splendid turban-clad inspector who told me, full of laughs and kind smiles, 'Oh, they be gone four weeks … more trouble than they was worth! …' (apparently they frequently knocked vital parts from their undersides in negotiating pedestrian-friendly crossing-ramps — a bit like playing with Hornby 'O'-gauge trains!) and, as an afterthought, 'Maybe they gone back to London or Scotland …'

But I wasn't going to visit London (too few RMs) or Scotland (too far, too expensive …) and I couldn't have reached Potter Heigham now, not even on a Sunday. And M and the South West Train had departed …

Above left: Norwich in mid August 2004 abounded in somewhat charming 1991/2 Dennis Darts with bodywork by Wrights of Ballymena, removed from London and now in FirstGroup corporate attire.

Right: And finally, back from the Norwich trip to Southampton; now bereft of bendi-buses, the scene doesn't look much different from Norwich — just more 'Barbie'.

Exposed in Edinburgh

It may be one of Britain's finest cities, but it certainly has never claimed to be the warmest. Yet over the last two decades Edinburgh has succumbed to the allure of open-top tour buses. BILLY NICOL dons warm clothing to capture a selection.

Above: Lothian's earliest open-toppers were Leyland Atlantean AN68s with Alexander bodies. One is seen leaving the Waverley Bridge departure point in 1993 in the original white, blue and black Edinburgh Classic Tour colours.

Above right: To replace the Atlanteans Lothian converted several of its Alexander-bodied Olympians, as shown by this 2000 view of a 1988 bus. It offers more protection for passengers and is in a brighter livery without the black skirt used originally.

Right: The early Olympians later received City Sightseeing livery, as shown on this vehicle on The Mound. Note the unusual location of the Lothian Buses fleetname — on the skirt ahead of the front wheel.

Left: Restriction on the operation of double-deckers in the city's parklands saw this former Western Scottish Leopard being used in 2000 on a tour marketed as The Royal Park Charabanc. It served Arthur's Seat and Salisbury Craggs. Like most Scottish Leopards it has an Alexander Y-type body.

Right: Exciting additions to the Lothian fleet in 2000 were four new open-toppers. These were Dennis Tridents with Plaxton President bodies and were the first brand-new permanently open-top double-deckers to-be built in Britain since the 1930s. When new they were in Edinburgh Classic Tour colours, but they were soon repainted in red City Sightseeing livery. One pauses outside Dynamic Earth.

Left: Mac Tours began city tours using old buses in 1999 and was purchased by Lothian in 2002. Mac's original and varied collection of half cab double-deckers was then replaced by 10 extended ERM-class Routemasters, identifiable by having five standard-length side windows instead of the four of the RMs on which they are based. Mac's livery is a smart red and cream.

Right: To provide more comfortable accommodation in inclement weather some of the Mac Tours Routemasters were partly re-roofed, as shown by this vehicle on the famous Royal Mile.

Left: For many years Guide Friday and Lothian competed for trade, but in 2002 Lothian acquired Guide Friday's operations in Scotland's capital. This is a 1988 Olympian, freshly repainted in pale green and cream. On this bus the full length of the roof has been removed, and a shallow windscreen fitted at the front of the upper deck.

Right: The Royal Yacht *Britannia*, moored at Leith, is one of Scotland's big visitor attractions, and in 2000 Lothian introduced a Britannia Tour, with a distinctive blue and yellow livery. In 2004 this was rebranded The Majestic Tour, as shown on this standard-length Routemaster at Waverley Bridge.